TODAY'S INSPIRED young LATINA

VOLUME II

INSPIRATION FROM YOUNG PROFESSIONAL LATINAS ACHIEVING THEIR DREAMS

Jacqueline S. Ruíz

Alexandria Ríos Taylor

TODAY'S INSPIRED YOUNG LATINA

© Copyright 2020, Fig Factor Media, LLC.
All rights reserved.

All rights reserved. No portion of this book may be reproduced by mechanical, photographic or electronic process, nor may it be stored in a retrieval system, transmitted in any form or otherwise be copied for public use or private use without written permission of the copyright owner.

This book is a compilation of stories from numerous people who have each contributed a chapter and is designed to provide inspiration to our readers.

It is sold with the understanding that the publisher and the individual authors are not engaged in the rendering of psychological, legal, accounting or other professional advice. The content and views in each chapter are the sole expression and opinion of its author and not necessarily the views of Fig Factor Media, LLC.

For more information, contact:

Jacqueline S. Ruiz
Fig Factor Media, LLC | www.figfactormedia.com
JJR Marketing, Inc. | www.jjrmarketing.com

Cover Design & Layout by Juan Pablo Ruiz
Printed in the United States of America

ISBN: 978-1-952779-14-5

Library of Congress Number: 2020943290

We dedicate this book to all of the authors and their families for their bravery in telling and sharing their stories. They've brought the seeds that we've been wanting to plant for access and opportunity around the world.

Table of Contents:

Acknowledgements 6

Introduction 7

Preface 11

JESSICA ZAMORA 19
    Defeating the Odds

CINDY FALLA-AGUADO 31
    In His Time

BERENICE DIAZ BAUTISTA 41
    My Journey to The Other Side

MAGDALENA GONZALEZ-HERNANDEZ 51
    Have Courage and Raise Up Your Voice

SANDRA LOPEZ 65
    Guerrera de mi Vida

CRISTINA RAMIREZ 77
    Back to Me

ALINE LAMADRID 89
    Beyond

MARISOL "PINQY RING" VELEZ 103
    "¿Nena, Otro Novio?" (Gurl... Anotha Man?!)

JANINE ARRIOLA 115
   Fear: I Love You, I Hate You, But Overall, I Thank You

LISSETE AGUIRRE OCHOA 127
   La Platicadora

KATERYN FERREIRA 137
   Diamonds Are Made Under Pressure

CLAUDIA GEORGINA MARTINEZ 149
   Mariposa

ARACELI DELEON-MENDEZ 163
   A Life of Decisions

AVELIRA GONZALEZ 177
   A Condo Downtown

BRENDA HERNANDEZ MARAVILLA 185
   Embracing Me

CRYSTAL ALINA PRUSEK 197
   Loving Myself So I Can Love Others

MIRIAM BIGURRA 209
   Mi Verdad

LUCERO CARRASCO 221
   A Different Education

Acknowledgements

We would like to thank all of the mentors, educators and business leaders who serve every day, and who have guided these beautiful women, set them upon a path to success, and paved the way in our community.

Thank you to our families for their love and patience.

Thank you to the Fig Factor Media team who made the impossible possible.

And thank you to Luz Canino-Baker for being a part of this project.

Introduction

When we began with *Today's Inspired Young Latina*, it was pure magic. It began as an event, turned into an amazing book, and evolved into a sisterhood for young women who told their stories and connected with those who read them. It was such an incredible experience that we knew there was room for it to grow and bloom into Volume II and inspire readers all over again.

We received wonderful feedback from the first volume and met young Latinas all over the country who wanted to know what happened "next"... what happens after walking across the stage on graduation day?.... then what?

We began to see the need to focus Volume II on life's transitional phase, on Latinas who are ready to bloom and blossom in all of their glory. "Blossom" can refer to a beautiful flower and the verb "to blossom" literally means to "flourish; to come into one's own". So this volume is dedicated to all of our Latinas who are blossoming, those who are moving into their first apartments, working in their first professional role, serving their country, getting married, starting college, buying their first car, having their first baby, or buying their first home. Each of these firsts are challenging but filled with so much magic and buds of growth. We remember this transitional time in our own lives, and in truth, looking back, get a bit nostalgic.

In this volume, we have chosen a very special group of young professional Latina women who are achieving their dreams and encouraging young readers to reach for the stars as they are also at the helm of life's biggest decisions. The magic of their message is the solidarity they offer YOU, our future Inspired Young Latina, as YOU evolve and move through your own transitional moments ahead, too!

Our co-authors' stories in this anthology are a magical blueprint of shared lived experiences that guide our next generation through all of the magical moments of each "first". Your soul will resonate with each voice and the familiarity in each chapter. You'll feel as though you are right there with them… inside each page, experiencing the journey as they do.

The sisterhood and resiliency that emerges from everyday struggles and victories provide a path forward and encourages all young Latinas to push through, continue moving, and make dreams happen! So come along on this ride with us! Read the stories from *hermanas* who know what it is like to live in your world. They ARE you, just a step ahead. They are vulnerable and fearless. Heed the lessons they offer, use them, and soar! Our collective hope is that this book inspires you to conquer defeats and emerge a victor, with a bit of fairy dust on your shoulders and flowers in your hand.

So are you ready to take the next step? Are you ready to fly? Are you ready to live your dreams, to change the world and your community, one person at a time? We know firsthand --it's an incredible feeling when the magic happens, when a friendship aligns, and when a passion project turns into our gift to you. It is our hope that you read each one of these stories, allow them to lead you, inspire you, and motivate you onward. We will be here cheering you on!

Love,

Alex and Jackie

God sometimes leads you on journeys that are not planned. If you are awake enough and alert enough to be cognizant of the messages that are being sent to your heart, those divine downloads, then you'll follow that path. For me, it's been following my gut, following my intuition, praying about it, and saying, what am I here to do? And then stopping to listen. Then I surprised myself at every turn, thinking how did I become a pioneer of Latino storytelling? But that's part of the magic. The moment we turned our stories into a book, it became a legacy. These young ladies are taking the awesome responsibility to share their stories, capture these moments in time forever, and light the way for other people. That's what elevating through authorship means.

~ Jacqueline S. Ruiz

I had no idea my life would come full-circle. As a student, I remember asking my high-school teacher if there were any books in our school library that had "me" in it? In our entire library, we had one book that represented the Latino community in a way that was uplifting and positive. It was a fiction book that transported me to a world where I belonged, albeit fantasy. Now, I'm grateful to be able to create a collection of real-life vignettes for all the young Latinas of the world who wish to see themselves represented and portrayed as triumphant. As a high school Assistant Principal, it is an awesome feeling to go into my own school library and offer my book whenever young Latinas request stories that positively reflect their own voices and community.

~ Alexandria Rios Taylor

Preface

BY ARGELIA ATILANO

Univision Talent and Radio Broadcaster

We all have a story to write, but it's not just about writing; it's also about sharing, listening, connecting, and relating. That is the main reason why I switched career paths during my college years and went from being a pre-law student to a communication studies major. It was during my time at Loyola Marymount University that I discovered the amazing sensation of feeling empowered by just hearing, and then retelling impactful, life-changing stories of painful adversity and huge triumph. I was nineteen years old when I woke up one morning, truly listening to my heart, and decided to follow my new ambition of pursuing journalism, without telling my family.

Not knowing if it was the smartest move, I took a risk and went with my instinct, even if it would mean taking out another student loan or staying an extra year. My mother was not completely happy with my choice (she dreamt of having a lawyer in the family), but after completing my four years as an undergraduate student, she was proud of the fact that one of her daughters became a first- generation college graduate in the family, leading a newfound path for the rest of my sisters to follow.

Fast forward twenty-five years and my mother continues to be my number one fan, followed by my two young daughters that get to turn on the radio every day and hear mommy's voice wake up thousands of people across the country in search of joy, a good dose of positive energy, and great laughs over a cup of coffee. Till this day I pinch myself and am grateful for having been able to read the signs that God sent me when I needed them the most. Still, how does a shy and fearful eight-year-old girl raised by a single mother with very little means grow up to be one of the most fearless, influential, and recognized voices of her own community? Little did I know back then that my journey would eventually lead me to co-host one of the most important morning radio shows in Los Angeles with the person who would later become my best friend and husband.

Together we have made history as a married couple on K-LOVE107.5 FM and have built a legacy by entertaining audiences for more than seventeen years. And just when we thought we had seen and said it all, a pandemic came, shook us to our core, caught us off guard, and knocked us down. Motivating our audience who is in desperate need of keeping their hope and faith alive has become our biggest challenge yet. More than a radio broadcaster, wife, mother, and daughter, I have to remind myself that I'm human first, therefore it's completely normal to feel helpless, insecure, fearful, and lost, like many of us are lately.

How did we get to where we are now? How did our lives turn upside down from one day to another? When did we begin to doubt ourselves and suddenly feel insecure all over again? How do we get out of this frazzled, lost, and confused state of mind? When do we start all over and how? To whom or what do we hang on to when times get tough? How or where does the motivator find motivation? All those questions and more still keep me up at night and yet, I don't have the answers. What I do know for sure is that when you're a person of faith like I am, we keep hanging on to God with all of our might, believing that he will indeed lighten up the load and show us the new way. Like the majority of us praying, fighting, and trying our very best to survive through a pandemic, I too have fallen on my knees feeling completely discouraged, questioning all of my life choices, career decisions, purpose in life, and reason for existence. However, when there is hope, we can cope. And right when I was hanging by a thread, ready to throw in the towel, take a break from it all and disappear for a while, I received a touching email from a young follower named Claudia Martinez, who with the power of her sweet words and brave story, took me back to my humble beginnings in Chicago, Illinois where my story began forty-five years ago.

I've always taken pride in saying that I was born in Chicago, raised in San Pedro, polished in San Juan de los Lagos, Jalisco, and reborn in East LA. I was only two years old when my parents decided to leave The Windy City for the Golden State of California. Besides Chicago being my birthplace, I really had no recollection or memory that tied me to my community of Chi-town...until now.

Little did I know that during the chaos and uncertainty of 2020, a wonderful beacon of hope called The Fig Factor Foundation, created by Jacqueline Ruiz, would come into my life to not only help me shake off the excess anxiety and accumulated stress consuming my spirit, but to also enlighten and fuel my soul by reminding me of the positive impact and the difference that my voice continues to make in the lives of aspiring young ladies. I can finally say that I have discovered a meaningful connection to my stomping grounds. Welcoming me into this beautiful community, whose members are beyond incredible and resilient young ladies, is an invitation that I will forever be grateful for. To know that my journey can be a source of inspiration adds true meaning to my purpose in life.

As I was getting to know the trials, tribulations, and breathtaking victories of each young lady as they poured every inch of their souls into the following pages, I was able to immediately identify with and relate to them.

The Lord works in mysterious ways. We just never know who, when, why, how and for what reason someone is going to come into our life, but when it does happen, we discover that a complete stranger has the power to open our eyes and change us forever. Had I not opened up that email from Claudia when I was feeling hopeless, I maybe wouldn't be here feeling hopeful, writing the preface for *Today's Inspired Young Latina Volume II*, a beautiful compilation of true testimonials that have the strength to inspire a five-year-old child or lift up a forty-five year old woman like me.

With the tense climate that we are all facing today, it is crucial and urgent that these stories get told and shared everywhere! Little girls from all walks of life, including my eleven and nine-year-old daughters need to know that they are standing on the shoulders of dreamers who have fought the good fight. The young women that we get to know in this collection are more than authors; they are extraordinary daughters and role models who have sacrificed and defied the odds with immeasurable courage in search of equal opportunities. More importantly, they are young warriors who have given all they've got in search of fulfilling their parent's mission as they pursued a life of profound happiness.

Marisol, "Fosforito," thank you for reminding us that true empowerment starts with self-love.

Claudia, you're absolutely correct; "there is always room to help others."

Janine, you are a brave and true hero that teaches us that fear has the power to push us to achieve bigger and greater things.

Aline, preach it proudly girl! My name is pronounced "R-he-lee-ah."

Lucero, I agree with you, school is not for everybody, but goals and aspirations are.

My "platicadora" **Lissete**, we will never be lost if we allow God to guide us on the path that he has designed for each and every one of us to take.

Traumatic events will make us or break us, but like **Cristina** has learned through her own journey, it's up to us to decide the outcome.

Sandra, you have inspired me to go back to my crib and nothing would make me happier than to meet you over a cup of coffee at your very own Cafeart Studio one day!

Magdalena, God bless our strong mothers, our number one fans fueling us with their love, endless support, sacrifices and loud chants of tu échale ganas which never fails!

Berenice, thank you for teaching us that a day without laughter is a day wasted. Life would not be the same without talented and spirited people like you!

Thank you, **Cindy**, for being a true manifestation of God's love.

Jessica, your wise words sum up the book beautifully. *"We all have a story that has shaped us to be who we are meant to be."* By sharing our individual stories, we realize that we truly are all connected through our life experiences, upbringing, traditions, values, and beliefs.

Kateryn, thank you for making us see that checking boxes and completing to do lists is not enough if we don't have appreciation, hope, faith, and courage in our heart.

Araceli you did not only find your true calling but along the way, you taught us that the path less chosen is in many ways, the right path.

Avelira's perseverance, hard work and achieved success is a true testament of our God-given talents that should not be defined by a test, but by true character and determination.

Brenda, you've discovered that the beauty of a journey is that it's never ending. Watch out world because you're just getting started!

If there is one thing that we can all learn during these trying times is to be more compassionate and kinder to ourselves. **Crystal**, you discovered the importance of that lesson and I thank you for sharing it with the rest of us.

Sometimes when we're feeling discouraged, all we need is a little push from someone or something to keep us on track, just like it happened to you, **Miriam**. Despite the challenges faced along the way, you are determined to not give up and that is your power!

Through these heartfelt and transparent stories, America's infinite possibilities of a better and fairer tomorrow are envisioned in this raw, candid, and honest book, destined to become an empowering guide for many little girls and women in search of self-love, self-identity, and self-discovery. To the shining stars within these pages, keep counting your blessings without losing sight of what you still need to accomplish in order to fulfill your true mission in life. Always take care of the best version of yourself, because nobody else will do it better than you. Continue your journey with honesty, integrity, confidence, determination, and trust in God, always. I know that your best life is yet to come, and I can't be more excited to see what the future holds for you. You just wait and see. It's your time.

Thank you for being light, hope and inspiration when it is needed most. I'm infinitely grateful to each of you for your stories of great determination, great heart, and tireless struggle. I'm excited to see them all shine, grow, conquer, and succeed even more!

Your fan forever,

Argelia Velasco Atilano
Univision Talent and Radio Broadcaster
K-Love 107.5 FM: El Show de Omar y Argelia

DEFEATING THE ODDS

Jessica Zamora

"Only when stigma is fully addressed can change truly happen."

At the tender age of six, my life took a pivotal turn. My parents separated and filed for divorce.

The change in our family dynamic was merely a fraction of the change I was about to face in my life. I had to transfer to a new school and relocate to a new neighborhood, which ultimately led my mother and I to move into my grandmother's house, where six other people were living.

SURVIVING DIVORCE

My new reality was reflective of my living environment: it was hurting. I lived in Little Village, commonly known as La Villita, a South Lawndale community on the west side of Chicago. It was tough not being able to see my dad every day, be without the comfort of the only home I knew, and be unable to play freely outside after school. I lived in the center hub of two rival gangs, where there was gun violence and a great deal of police activity. After a homicide occurred on the front steps of our house, I was limited to playing indoors and sometimes in the backyard. I felt constrained and unable to thrive.

There were countless occasions my first-grade teacher would find me hiding in the closet of the classroom, crying tirelessly. I isolated myself from the rest of the other students, and the closet was that safe space to release the emotions I felt. To say that I was overwhelmed by all the changes happening simultaneously was an understatement; I was an only child going through these transitions alone and that made it that much more challenging to cope with my situation.

My status as "daddy's little girl," when I felt on top of the world, was now a distant memory. My father-daughter relationship grew ever more distant after the divorce. There were months at a time I did not see him and he was not there to celebrate my birthday or other special occasions. On visitation days, when we were scheduled to get together, it often did not go as planned. I remember early one Sunday morning, I got dressed as fast as I could for an eventful day with him. I was ecstatic to dine at my favorite breakfast place and go to the theater to see a new, anticipated movie. I sat on the couch in the living room, looking out the window and trying to spot my dad's car amid the others. My 15-minute wait turned into hours, sitting in the exact same spot until dark. These reoccurring instances plummeted my confidence and made me wonder if there was something about me that was not good enough. My dad would call and apologize for not showing up due to unforeseen circumstances, but his reasons never filled that void of missing out on another day of spending quality time with him.

Ironically, I would often come home quite frustrated on the days we would spend time together because I was put in the position of acting as a messenger between my father and mother. I didn't know anything about their financial arrangements and yet I was engaging in these awkward conversations. I never seemed to have the correct opinion or defend the right parent, and I ultimately became an outlet for my parent's frustrations. I was even more frustrated when I had to have these conversations in public. It was embarrassing to have my family's private affairs broadcasted in front of strangers and this took a toll on me and made me a temperamental child. I felt "stuck," and unable to help with these serious, adult issues.

During this time, my mother was a single parent juggling full-time employment while pursuing her undergraduate studies. She witnessed how these transitions affected me emotionally and mentally and did her best to provide me with the support I needed. My mom feared these transitions would deprive me of reaching my highest potential, so she had me involved in an array of extracurricular activities like piano classes, swimming lessons, and an after-school program for inner city girls called Metro Achievement Center. For ten years, I formed part of the Metro family where I received mentorship and one-to-one tutoring. I began to form new friendships outside of school and I developed confidence in myself to tackle difficult subjects. I was happy to see an improvement in my academics. It was a time I truly began to branch out and thrive in my environment. And it was only the beginning.

When I turned twelve, I developed a great sense of self-love that sparked self-confidence within me I never knew I had. I was recruited by John Robert Powers, a modeling agency in downtown Chicago, where I was featured in photoshoots, commercials, and I learned a great deal about fashion. I naturally posed for pictures and had a way of modeling gracefully. I loved to be in front of a camera and have a platform where I could express my authenticity without regard. This was empowering!

To my surprise, I inherited the gene for modeling from my mother, who participated in the industry in her teenage years. Although my dad was not present to share in some of my successes, my mother's guidance and love ignited a fire of confidence within me that made me believe I could do whatever I set out to do, despite any barriers and challenges. My mother always said that when there is discomfort, growth happens the most and when others doubt in my capability, I should use that as fuel to continue moving forward. With my mother's blessing, that is exactly what I did.

FLYING HIGH IN HIGH SCHOOL

In my freshman year of high school, l made the decision to join the debate team as an extemporancous speaker. I vividly remember spending countless hours after school researching articles on a range of topics like health, politics, and education related to Latinos in the United States. Based on a given question, I would have to utilize those resources to support claims made in pro and counter arguments that all had to be written in under thirty minutes. It was the call of the judges to decide if I had to debate my pro or counter argument. Although the debate itself was fifteen minutes followed by Q& A, the process to get to that point was the most nerve-wracking of it all. I had to learn to think quickly on my feet and answer questions using prior knowledge of my research. Round after round of practice, I began to gain confidence in my capabilities. Eventually, I was fully prepared for the most anticipated event, the Midwest Great Debate. It was intimidating to be in a room full of other talented Latino students from across the Chicagoland area. Despite how difficult each round of debate became, I stayed authentic to my style of delivery. I was recognized as a semi-finalist! I believe that if it weren't for my mother's support throughout the entire process, that would not have been possible.

The experience pushed me out of my comfort zone in unimaginable ways. For the first time, I felt confident in my writing abilities, public speaking, and was no longer that shy child afraid to vocalize her opinions. I couldn't be more grateful. This aspired to bigger dreams. The following year, in 2007, I studied abroad in Beijing, China for a month. I was only sixteen years old, and my parents were afraid to let me leave the country and explore the other side of the world on my own. I did have weekend traditions of dining in Chinatown and watching Bruce Lee movies with my father, which gave me an Americanized glimpse into the culture, but I wanted to take a deeper dive.

After much hesitation from my parents, I was given the green light and I couldn't have been more ecstatic. For me, it was a dream come true to travel abroad and immerse myself in a new culture. I learned conversational Mandarin, explored historical landmarks, and indulged in traditional dishes. It was a lifetime opportunity to live with a host family and be exposed to beautiful customs and traditions that only broadened my understanding of the culture. In 2019, after eleven years, I even reunited with my host family in Beijing. I was welcomed with open arms the same way I was first received into the country. I now have a new home in Beijing and for that I couldn't be more grateful.

The highlights in my high school career were more than just personal accomplishments; they helped develop my character, which helped define my own brand. Truthfully, my upbringing also shaped me into who I am today. In adolescence, it was difficult to comprehend my circumstances, but as I have reached adulthood, I see now that my childhood shaped me into a strong-minded, self-assured woman. Having my father as a presence in my adulthood has also made the transition easier. It has filled that void I had felt as a child for so long.

HELPING THOSE WHO NEED HELP

Since high school, I have aspired to promote better health outcomes in disadvantaged communities impacted by preventable, chronic illnesses. The course of my education, work history, and upbringing has created a pathway to develop and accomplish what I want to do as a public health professional. As a woman of color navigating the world, this has become my cape and armor.

For two consecutive years, I was denied acceptance to graduate school. This is not something I have openly shared with anyone because at the time, I did feel defeated, but was still determined to prove that I was good enough and deserving to be in the program. After submitting my application for the third year, I was accepted to the University of Illinois at Chicago and completed one of the top public health programs in the country. Without the support and mentorship of my mother, this also would not have been possible.

As a child, I promised my mother I would not allow myself to become a single parent statistic. Studies say that children from unconventional homes are at-risk of being pushed out from high school, teenage pregnancy, and not attending college. I wanted to defeat the odds. It became my mission to redefine what a child from a "broken home" looked like, especially for a first-generation, Mexican-American who already had to overcome pre-existing challenges. This mission gave me the resilience to reframe my failures as lessons for adulthood. Defeating the odds was not just a phrase I would use to keep up momentum; it was a movement to celebrate accomplishments that further deterred me from becoming a statistic. I did everything I could to stay true to that promise.

For the past five years, I have committed myself to improving the health of populations impacted by HIV/AIDS. After receiving my certification for HIV testing and counseling, I began to administer confidential testing and counseling to high risk groups within underserved communities across the Chicagoland area. These individuals are persons who are affected by homelessness, addiction, and mental health concerns. I currently provide care coordination to persons living with HIV. I assure their access to social services as a means to address their social barriers to care.

I practice cultural competency, a practice of being non-judgmental and understanding when I speak to patients. It's a way of forging trusting relationships and rapport that creates a safe space for patients and clients to openly express their concerns and feel understood. This practice helps promote attendance to follow-up care appointments and compliance to their medical regimen. It's truly rewarding to come home every day from work, knowing I made a difference, however large or small, in someone's life. It has been priceless to witness the journey of my patients from being very ill to becoming advocates for their own individual, healthcare needs.

Outside of work, however, many do not understand what I do. Sometimes I feel misunderstood; many have expressed fear for my well-being for working with this vulnerable population. I have used those opportunities to enlighten, educate, and debunk the myths surrounding the etiology and transmission of the disease. Sometimes it works; sometimes it doesn't.

A strong stigma persists in our society which is the root cause of poor health and inequities among the homeless, addicted, and mentally ill. There is still a lot of work needed to be done to address it. There are many misconceptions about HIV, and we need to improve and promote health education, especially among sexual, gender, and ethnic minorities who are disproportionately affected.

I'm disappointed that in most homes, the discussion of sexual health is a taboo topic, yet sex is manifested in so many ways in the media like music, telenovelas, and movies. As a Mexican-American from a Catholic household, I know this is true. I did not have the talk about the birds and the bees but was educated on the importance of staying pure and untouched until I was married. I remember my grandmother attempting to give me a lesson on virginity.

"You see this clean glass cup?" she asked.

"Yes," I replied.

"See what happens when I touch it? My fingerprints are on it now. This cup is no longer clean because it is touched. When a man touches you, you are no longer clean."

This lesson reminds me of an episode of Jane the Virgin when abuela demonstrates to Jane how rose petals can no longer restore their original state once they are touched. These lessons demonstrate that the decision to become intimate should not be taken lightly, but it lacks an introduction to healthy, safe practices that can reduce HIV and other sexually transmitted infections. In my career, I have tried to find effective approaches to address the stigma of testing for HIV and other sexually transmitted infections. In both the Latino and African American communities, I have conducted sexual health education workshops and distributed resources about the importance of knowing your status. There are many who have ingrained beliefs about what an at-risk person for these infections "looks like." These misconceptions become barriers to effectively promote sex education and a reason why many continue to become infected. Only when stigma is fully addressed can change truly happen.

As a child from a single-family home and a less than ideal community, I overcame the obstacles in my path due to support and guidance from my mother. In the same way, I want to be that helping hand of support to empower the populations I serve. My patients live in less than ideal circumstances, and all they need is guidance and support from someone. Many do not have trusted friends and lack familial support because of their HIV status. Many are afraid to disclose their status because they fear they will be "abandoned" by their family and friends. It is reassuring when my patients tell me how they appreciate all I do for them and wouldn't be where they are without that support. It is a priceless feeling to provide patients the resources to help them lead a better quality of life and achieve good health.

THINK YOUNG AND GROW

My challenge to you is to not judge a book by its cover. As cliché as that may sound, technology has made it easy to connect and disconnect with people from the outside world. Our own personal biases about the way a person looks, dresses, and acts can get in the way of making a genuine connection that can possibly lead to a lifetime friendship or partnership. Being non-judgmental and getting to know that person for who they are can give a greater insight into why they are the way that they are. Everyone has a story, and that has shaped them to be who they are today. It does not matter what religion, ethnicity, gender identity, sexual orientation, or HIV status they have. At the end of the day we are all human, trying to make a connection in this world.

I can assure you that after you engage with someone you normally wouldn't, your perspective will change. You may discover that there is a shared passion for cooking, reading, or love for binge-worthy shows. If that interaction allows you to get into a deeper conversation, you may discover you have had to overcome similar challenges or defeat similar odds. All it takes is open-mindedness to allow that opportunity to flourish. Then personal growth truly happens, and the world becomes a better place.

THIS IS ME

My name is Jessica Zamora and I am a recent Master of Public Health graduate from the University of Illinois at Chicago (UIC) and a board member for The Latino Caucus for Public Health (LCPH). I received my B.S. in Community Health Sciences from the University of Illinois-Urbana-Champaign. For the past five years, I have worked in the HIV sector. After working in communities across the Chicagoland area conducting HIV testing and health education, I now spearhead a care coordination project for persons living with HIV/AIDS at Ruth M. Rothstein CORE Center, the largest HIV treatment facility in the Midwest. My passion for the public health field given me the opportunity to instruct a community health course for youth at the UIC Early Outreach Program and perform research at the World Health Organization (WHO) in Geneva, Switzerland.

 *My dream is to change how society views and perceives disease. I aspire to lead a public health program that can prevent and control the spread of infectious disease to protect public health.*

THE FIVE-YEAR PLAN

1. Complete a fellowship program with the Centers for Disease Control and Prevention
2. Learn fluent Mandarin
3. Relocate to Geneva, Switzerland and work for the World Health Organization

IN HIS TIME

Cindy Falla-Aguado

"Trust in Him. His plan and timing are perfect."

I was eight years old and living in Miami. I am a preacher's kid, or PK as they say. I am the youngest of three siblings who are a decade older than me, so I pretty much had two sets of parents. It had its perks at times. We stayed in Miami where my parents planted a church. They were pastors but also had to work in factories and deliver newspapers for additional income. Those jobs were tough, but sacrifices had to be made to pastor the church. I was with my dad often and known as his *compañera fiel*, or faithful companion.

    I loved the sun and the playground next to my house. I was always on my bike, climbing trees, and organizing the neighborhood shows starring myself with my "cool" gymnastics moves. I enjoyed school and church but above all, I loved being around babies. I enjoyed feeding them, playing with them, and pretending to be their mom. I would always help in the church's infant and toddler room. At the age of ten, I became an aunt to a beautiful boy, Gabriel. His name was originally going to be Joshua but at the last minute they changed it. I decided then and there that if I had a boy of my own, I would name him Joshua.

On June 5, 1995, I carried baby Gabriel in my arms for the first time and I instantly knew that my goal in life was to be a mother. I wanted to help my sister take care of him, but I thought it was also good practice for me. I would wake up at four o'clock in the morning, get his bottle ready, change his diaper, and put him back to sleep. I would pretend to be his mom, and I was in love with that feeling.

COLOMBIA AND BACK

Then, my parents followed the call of ministry and were getting us ready for a big move. We were going to Colombia, where my parents are originally from, to serve as missionaries. Although they were ready to work full time doing God's work, life as I knew it would never be the same. We were going in a new direction and only God knew the plan.

In 1995, we arrived in Bogota, Colombia. I was ten years old. My sister moved there with her husband and my nephew, Gabriel. I was so excited to see them but not at all excited to be in Colombia. My Spanish was not great, and I did not have friends there. Colombia was also still dangerous because of the drug lords and Guerrillas, although not as bad as it once was. Regardless, my parents didn't want me to speak English in public because they feared for my safety. That was hard for me. I felt like a prisoner in my own body.

Because of my language barrier and for my safety, I was enrolled in a bilingual private school where all the kids were wealthy. It was overwhelming, and I felt out of place. On my entrance exam, they gave me a geography and history test based on Colombia. I thought to myself, *"How am I supposed to know this? I'm not from here."* I ended up failing. So even though I was supposed to start my new school as a seventh grader, I was demoted to the fifth grade. It was humiliating and unfair.

Since I obviously did not fit in with the kids in the fifth grade and the seventh graders didn't like me, I started to hang out with the tenth graders. I started to act older than I actually was, maybe because I grew up around older people. I wanted to fit, in so I started playing volleyball, joined the cheerleading squad and got involved in theater. Eventually, things got a little better.

When I was fourteen, I transferred to a Christian school with all Spanish-speaking classes. It was still a private school but not as wealthy. I felt more comfortable there and made great friends. I loved my teachers, and it was a good time in my life. But just as I was getting settled, my life was uprooted again.

After years in mission work, my parents took a one-year sabbatical. We had to go back to the U.S. and leave my home, my friends, and my comfort, again. I had fallen in love with Colombia; not sure when it happened, but now I suddenly did not want to leave. I was sixteen years old and in a serious relationship, which eventually ended because of my immaturity and distance. Then during our sabbatical, the unthinkable happened. The tragedy of September 11 hit. I had never felt so sad or cried so much. I was heartbroken and all I could do was pray. The devastation brought perspective, and I decided to live life fully. I decided to go back to Colombia on my own and finish school.

At seventeen, I was almost completely independent. I was doing well in school, spent time with my old friends and made some new ones. I fell in love, but it was a one-sided relationship that was never meant to last. The day we broke up, I cried and prayed that God would someday give me a husband just like my dad; a man who would love God and me unconditionally. I wanted a stable and beautiful marriage, like my parents had.

BABY LOVE

I needed new energy and went to Miami to meet my new, beautiful niece, Juliana. It was refreshing. Most people my age would be annoyed by a baby, but not me. My spirit was happy to have a baby in the room; a baby I could feed, change, and hold while my sister rested. Once again, I loved playing mom. I learned to multitask and was quite a natural. I was in a restaurant, simultaneously feeding my niece her bottle while eating when someone told me my daughter looked a lot like me. I was over the moon that I was mistaken for being her mother. Of course, my sister corrected them immediately, but I didn't care. At that moment, "I looked like a mom," and I knew I would make a great mother someday and if God could bless me with twins, even better.

Once we got back to Colombia, I got my GED so I wouldn't

have to return to school. Soon, I would have to choose a major for college and I had no idea what to pursue. I desperately wished there was a major called, "How to be a wife and mother." That is all I really wanted to be. But since that wasn't an option, I went to school to be a physical therapist. I loved helping people and I knew I could still work with kids, so it was the perfect profession.

By the end of my freshmen year, I was in a new, wonderfully stable relationship. I even thought that he might be "the one." Shortly thereafter, I decided to spend Christmas and New Years with my brother in Chicago. I ended up meeting one of his best friends who was tall, funny, and had the most beautiful green eyes. He also happened to be a Christian with parents who were pastors. Although there were many similarities and lots of chemistry, we remained just friends. I was in a committed relationship and lived in another country. I went back home.

Three years went by and it was time for me to graduate. Even though my relationship had become unhealthy (lots of break-ups and fights), I wanted to be a wife and mother badly enough that I said "yes" to an engagement. It lasted just two months. My plans were not going as I wanted.

I promised my parents I would return to Chicago after graduation and pursue my career, so I did. I worked as a chiropractic assistant, on my own, paying rent, and covering most of my expenses. The transition from living in Colombia to living in Chicago came with a culture shock. I had my family around to help me but someone else started coming around too. Remember the tall, handsome guy with the green eyes? He was suddenly in my life again.

GOD'S PLAN

At first, my brother not too happy about us being together (since they were best friends). But his friend became my knight in shining armor. I told my brother about the prayer I made when I was seventeen and we both knew that he was the one. He would pick me up in his red Honda Civic with the loudest sounding muffler ever. He would take me to interviews, bring me lunch, surprise me with gifts, take me out dancing, and be available when I felt scared and alone in my apartment. No matter the place or time, he was there. He courted me properly and made his intentions known. He was the husband I prayed for, the one that had my dad's characteristics, and the one who loved God. He was patient, calm, passionate, and protective. It's not a coincidence that he also had my father's name, Gamaliel, which is not a very common name. When it came to the people he loved and his beliefs, he was firm. After just two months of dating, he proposed on Thanksgiving Day in front of both of our families. Six months later, on May 29, 2009, we were married, with both of our parents performing the ceremony.

Then, two things happened. First, my career as a physical therapist met an unexpected challenge. I found out that my Colombian certifications would not transfer, and I would have to be recertified to practice physical therapy in the U.S. Also, I need to resubmit my Colombian school transcripts which had to be translated and new credits needed to be applied to them, in addition to other requirements. It was crushing.

But my heart lifted when in October of the following year,

my son was born, and we named him Joshua Gamaliel. The baby that I desperately wanted since I was ten years old was finally in my arms. I did not have to pretend anymore. I did not have to give him up after watching him for a night. He was all mine. God had heard me and answered my prayers. I was so happy. I waited and, on His time, and on His terms, he granted me the true desire of my heart.

When Joshua was three years old, I went to a fertility doctor to make sure everything was okay because I wanted a second child but was not getting pregnant. After a little help, we conceived and on one of the saddest days of the year for me, September 11, the most beautiful girl with hazel eyes was born. That day now brings me such joy, thanks to Amanda, my second child.

Life after two kids was chaotic, but perfect. I still felt badly, however, for not finishing my physical therapy certifications sooner. I knew it was time to go back to school and I was determined to finish my required credits and prove that working mothers can do it all. While I was finishing the last twenty credits to receive my degree, God gave me the biggest unexpected blessing of all: I found out I was pregnant with twin girls, Annabelle, and Alannah. Although I had secretly prayed for twins, nothing could prepare me for the moment I saw the ultrasound with "Baby A" and "Baby B." My newfound career as a wife and mother was my priority and my answered prayer. Even still, I worked hard to finish my schooling before the twins were born so that when the moment is right, my future career awaits.

What I learned from my experiences with career and

motherhood is that a career is something we devote ourselves to for a season. It's something worthy enough of our energy, skill set, and time. It's a job that enriches our lives and those around us. Certainly, motherhood meets those criteria too. Today, my career is demanding. I work long days, overtime, nights, and weekends. My bonuses are smiles and hugs. My income is the fruit of my work in instilling values and convictions within my children that I see them demonstrate daily. Growing up to be a mom and wife is something to be proud of and applauded. Caring for others is the hardest job to do and also the most rewarding. It means I am entrusted with the total responsibility for the health, morals, emotional strengths, attitudes, discipline, and success of little ones. It's what I'm called to do and what I'm great at.

Although I can always go back to physical therapy when the time is right, I realized that I'm actually already operating in that role right now. When you look up the definition of a physical therapist, it is an "expert who optimizes quality of life through exercise, hands-on care, and education." This, my friends, is God letting me know that this was all part of His plan. Trust in Him. His plan and timing are perfect.

THINK YOUNG AND GROW!

Stay true to the vision YOU have for your future. Even if your vision and your future doesn't look like it "should," it's okay because the day you get there, you'll see how enormously happy you are. I encourage you to trust, pray, and write down your petitions of what you want in faith. Trust in him. Be specific, think about and list:

1. The marriage you want
2. The vision you have for your children
3. The job you dream about
4. The house you want to buy
5. The trip you want to take

But do not forget that God's will is perfect and sometimes what we want is not what he may want for us, but He foresees it all. Keep your heart and mind open to all the possibilities he has to offer.

Now know, trust, and pray that "When the time is right, I, the Lord will make it happen."- Isaiah 60:22.

THIS IS ME

My name is Cindy Falla-Aguado. I am blessed to be married to the perfect man God made for me, Gamaliel Aguado. I am mother to nine-year-old boy Joshua, five-year-old Amanda, and four-year-old twins, Annabelle and Alannah. Although I am a wife, daughter, sister, and friend, the most important people in my life call me "mommy" and "tia." I'm also a P.K. (preacher's kid) and a Christian. I'm a leader of three Christian women's book clubs and an active member with ministry at my church, Comunidad Cristiana (un lugar seguro) in Joliet, Illinois. IL.

One day I would like to be my own boss, have my own podcast on motherhood and marriage, write a book, and be a part of a nonprofit organization combating human trafficking.

THE FIVE-YEAR PLAN

1. Go international with my own podcast
2. Buy my dream house
3. Complete the Ultra-Spartan race (a 50K run with 60 obstacles)

MY JOURNEY TO THE OTHER SIDE

Berenice Diaz Bautista

"Just be yourself and to let go of people's negativity "

I was sitting down on the pavement, eating a big bag of spicy Cheetos on a hot, sunny day in Morelos, Mexico. By my side there was a stack of topos, little toys that came out of the Cheeto bags. I was saving them to trade with my brother, sister, and uncle, and daydreaming of the new life we were going to have once we left Mexico and headed to the United States to reunite with my parents.

A MEMORABLE JOURNEY

I asked my uncle, *"Me puedo llevar estos topos a los Estados Unidos"* ("Can I take these toys to the United States?") He answered, *"No Bere, mañana te vas."* ("You leave tomorrow, plus the border patrol police guys will take them away from you!")

All I remember was hiding three little topos in my backpack to keep me safe. So many thoughts were rushing through my head at that moment. Who was the border patrol and why did we have to encounter them? Everything was so unclear at the age of five but it made me happy to know I would be seeing my parents again. But to do it, I had to leave everything behind—my childhood friends and my grandma.

My grandma, Mama Chole, took care of us for a whole year while my hardworking immigrant parents chased that American dream *al otro lado de la frontera* (on the other side of the border). When I started my journey to the U.S., I took one pair of clothes, the pair of shoes I was wearing, and a gallon of water stuffed in a little backpack. This was not a normal childhood journey; it was something I remember to this day.

Taking the treacherous journey were my three-year-old sister, my four-year-old brother, my godparents, and me. We walked a bit through the desert in Nogales, to get to a van which would take us to U.S. soil. There were about fifteen other people who were headed to the United States that night. The only noise we could hear was our own footsteps and the empty, windy desert. I was holding my godmother's hand while she and my godfather carried my siblings. The night was very chilly, and I was super sleepy. I would look up into the sky and see the big moon shining and lighting up the desert, and it gave me comfort. Something told me I was safe.

But above us in the sky, there was a big black and white helicopter with a blinding spotlight, combing the desert to reveal people making the crossing. When the spotlight began sweeping our group, we suddenly heard a command from the sky, "EVERYONE GET DOWN! AND DON'T MOVE!" The helicopter was now only twenty feet off the ground, hovering above us, and our group began shouting and crying for everyone to hide. At that moment, I started having a panic attack. My heart was racing, my chest started to tighten up making it hard to breathe, and I was sweating at the same time. I was holding my little brother's hand, but at one point he let go because my godmother pulled him aside to hide in some brush, because there were border patrol trucks coming our way. Meanwhile, my godfather grabbed me and covered my mouth. Tears were rolling down my cheeks. Nothing could describe the terror I felt that instant. All I had was my godfather, holding me close, crouched in hiding, whispering that everything was going to be ok. I watched the border patrol take my godmother, my brother and my sister into custody. I was horrified. Would I ever see them again? "Don't worry *Mija*, you will see them tomorrow," my Godfather whispered, trying to soothe me. We were lucky. They could not take us all and we had hidden well.

After the border patrol left, the "coyotes" came to help us. They were the experts at smuggling people across the U.S.-Mexico border. They helped us move quickly to a white van and we left for our resting place. We had to wait two days in Arizona in an abandoned house waiting for my siblings and the other people traveling with us. The house was secluded and smelled musty, stale, and smoky at the same time. Several families were there, resting on the floor with coyotes talking to them about money and food. "*Estamos en tierra Americana vieja!*" ("We are on American soil, wifey") a guy was saying to his wife. You could tell by his face that he was so happy to be there.

Luckily, I did see my brother and sister again two days later. Some people had to swim through the Rio Grande to get to the other side. Not everyone survives those deadly waters, as you can imagine. Like I said, this was not a normal journey, but in the end it was rewarding. My siblings, godparents, and I got in a car driven by the coyotes to get to the Arizona airport headed to Midway Airport in Chicago. Then we headed on to a little town called Prospect Heights, Illinois to be reunited with our parents. I don't remember much after the car ride because we all slept through it. After all, we were super exhausted from the whole trip.

AN AMERICAN TEEN

Coming to the U.S. to chase *El Sueño Americano*, or the so-called American Dream, was a life-changing experience. I learned a whole new language and received opportunities that I never would have gotten in Mexico. Yes, our family struggled a lot, but we were able to start a better life. There are approximately eleven million undocumented people in the U.S. and immigration has been a big issue ever since I can remember.

"Invisibility, it starts with you, we can't afford to wait for the world to be equal to start being seen. We're far from it. Time will not allow it. You got to find the tools within yourself to feel visible, to be heard and to use your voice" Michelle Obama once said on her *Becoming* book tour. Those words stuck to me till this day since we're the only ones who can change our future and happiness.

Here in the U.S. I learned to have gratitude, openness to experiences, stand my ground, and be super "woke" about everything. My neighborhood in Prospect Heights was called Piper Lane. "The ghetto," as other kids and people called it. But that "ghetto" helped me stay awake and appreciate the little things in life.

I saw both my parents work two jobs, day and night, nonstop, to provide food, clothes, and a roof over our heads to make ends meet. I appreciated it because many kids I knew were joining gangs and leaving school. I promised myself I would be different, so I took the initiative to stay busy and let my brother and sister tagalong with me.

I guess I was like their second mom because I would always chase them around *como una gallina sin cabeza* (like a chicken with its head cut off!) I made sure to get up two hours early to make it on time to places. If not, we would fall into that cliche of running on Mexican time! I would take advantage of the after-school programs and clubs, and would also head to the Indian Trails Library to do my homework and use their computers.

I can say I have an outgoing and bubbly personality and I was always surrounded by friends and very social. I had decent grades and I was a step ahead of everyone else. Society was setting me up for failure based on how and where I lived, but I had bigger plans in mind… to succeed. My parents would always tell us *"Echale Gana mija, no se queden atrás, tenemos que avanzar en esta vida."* (Go for it, push through, don't get caught behind, we need to advance in life.")

I don't regret all the experiences I had in Piper Lane because it gave me character. I also give a big shout out to District 21 schools, in particular, Robert Frost Elementary and Holmes Middle School, for blessing us with clothing and food when we were in need of them. Also, thank you to Bertha Sanchez, Ana Molina, and Gaby Medina, my mentors throughout Wheeling High School, for always pushing me to graduate, get good grades, and get started on college applications.

Since I'm first-generation in the U.S. and the first person in my family to go to college, it was difficult for me to focus and apply to college on my own since my parents had no clue about it. I want to thank the outreach programs that the Prospect Heights police offered during the summer. They were very helpful and kept us out of trouble by taking us on adventures throughout Chicago. I know for a fact that one day I will be giving back to my community and making an impact like they did for us.

Then, on August 15, 2012, President Barack Obama signed an executive order that provided some level of relief from deportation to children who arrived in the United States at a young age. DACA (Deferred Action for Childhood Arrivals) was a cause for celebration for me. I finally got a work permit and was able to pursue higher education and get a driver's license. Throughout high school, I was teased for not taking the behind the wheel class and I would cry to my parents, miserable that I had not been born in the U.S. Now, I was no longer hiding in the shadows or scared to drive.

It was a powerful, new beginning that really helped me after graduation. Although this may be true now, looking back at it, it was silly for me to say I was proud to be Mexican and overcome those obstacles. My advice is to just be yourself and to let go of people's negativity. They will always talk.

THE AMERICAN DREAM

I had a difficult time with family struggles and transitioning to becoming an adult after high school. I wasn't sure what career I wanted but I was pressured to take my general education credits at nearby William Rayne Harper College while I figured it out. I was studying to become a bilingual teacher because I loved being a mentor and teaching the little ones, but something in me wanted more.

Growing up, I loved watching movies and novellas with my mom. I would always rent out ten movies maximum from the library and reenact scenes. I know it sounded crazy, but I would tell everyone that one day I would be on TV. While I was working two jobs and going to school, I would sneak out and take acting, singing, and dancing classes in my free time without my mom knowing. She wanted me to get a "real job" but that didn't stop me. I was so stressed out that I stopped going to school and focused on saving money. About that time, I met a wonderful lady named Jackie Camacho through a friend and I got the opportunity to join the Fig Factor Foundation as part of Core 2.

The Fig Factor helped me in many ways. I had a mentor for six months who still today is like a second mom to me! Luz-Marie Caro, you are appreciated. I became a great leader in the Latina community and followed my dreams because my mentors believed in me. You know what they say; it only takes one person to believe in you and make great things happen.

It's not easy being a modern-day Latina, but in order to be the best I can be I need to be fearless in whatever obstacles I face. In 2016, I took a leap of faith and followed my dream of pursuing an acting career by moving to Los Angeles, California. I had a vision and I was going to make it happen.

I applied to several schools and I got into one. I had two weeks to conclude my life in Chicago and start school at the Theatre of Arts College for the Contemporary Actor in Hollywood, California. I packed my bags and dreams into my little Toyota Corolla and drove two thousand, two hundred and seventy-six miles and three full days to California to start a whole new life. I'm not going to lie; these three years I've been in California have been a rollercoaster, with good and bad things happening to me. I went from having money saved to having no money, working part-time, making ends meet, and paying my tuition. Looking back, despite where I came from, I didn't give up. *Yo soy una Guerrera*. (I am a warrior).

It was difficult being alone in a new state where I didn't know anyone and had no family to rely on. I am grateful for the Bello-Jimenez family for helping me out with housing and food. To this day I do standup comedy, perform theatre, and do acting. I know I am destined for great things! I also want to thank David Conolly for being a great comedy mentor and for believing in me through my comedy career.

Coming to the U.S. was a life-changing experience, *El Sueño Americano*, or the so-called American Dream. I learned a whole new language and received opportunities that I never would have gotten in Mexico. Yes, our family struggled a lot but we were able to start a better life. There are approximately eleven million undocumented people in the U.S. and immigration has been a big issue ever since I can remember.

Our President encourages hatred towards our community and others, but that doesn't stop me. Like everyone here, I work a day to day job and pay taxes. I can tell you from experience, I am following my goals and ambitions for everyone to see. WE ARE HERE TO STAY! *(AQUI NOS QUEDAMOS MI GENTE!)*

THINK YOUNG AND GROW

All my life I have had mentors who have taught me because my parents weren't around much when I was growing up. When fear, anxiety, and self-doubt would creep in, I would seek inspiration from others through groups or self-help books. Try reading *"The Artist's Way"* by Julia Cameron. It's a spiritual path to higher creativity.

If you don't know where to begin a new journey, I recommend three things:

1. **Keep a journal next to your bed and start doing morning pages to get into your morning flow and creativity.** Write down any idea or worry in your head. I did this for months and found myself creating new standup jokes or ideas of little sketches I want to film. My morning pages also leave all my built-up negativity in my journal.
2. **Write down your short-term goals.** I tend to do month-

to-month goals so I can focus on the NOW and not what's going to happen later. I have learned to describe my relationship with time as if it were a person. This really helps me focus, get things done, and be more realistic about my priorities.
3. **Keep a calendar handy wherever you go**--in your room, on your phone, in your car. This will help you stay organized and focus on your day-to-day work.

THIS IS ME

I am Berenice Diaz Bautista. I am a hardworking Latina who was born in Iguala Guerrero, Mexico but raised in Prospect Heights, Illinois. I work in customer service and in my free time I like to volunteer at outreach programs and fight for human rights. When I'm not working my full-time job, I hit up comedy clubs in Los Angeles and perform stand-up comedy. I also audition as much as possible for roles or commercials. I know that one day my hard work will pay off.

I aspire to be a working actress on a Netflix series or a feature film in comedy and also work on stand-up and improv as well.

THE FIVE-YEAR PLAN

1. Become financially stable, retire my parents and travel
2. Write inspirational books and help LatinX communities
3. Earn an acting/comedy award for my craft

ÉCHALE GANAS Y HAZ TU VOZ BRILLAR
HAVE COURAGE AND RAISE UP YOUR VOICE

Magdalena Gonzalez Hernandez

"Have courage. Rise from the shadows. Conquer your fears."

What do you fear most?

For me, I fear losing my voice, being censored, and unable to fight for what I deserve. I fear losing control over everything I have worked so hard to obtain: the life I have created here in this country, the friendships I cherish, the nuclear family I support financially and emotionally, my purpose, and my career, which has just begun to bloom. I am frightened that one day, all of it will be gone in the blink of an eye and my life as I know it will unravel uncontrollably like a loose thread from a sweater. Worst of all, I fear being separated from my family. I live in fear that one day, I will arrive home and find Immigration and Customs Enforcement (ICE) officials waiting to take me to a deportation center. I am afraid of being treated as less than a human because as a DACA recipient, I lack citizenship status.

More than six hundred thousand DACA undocumented youth face this alarming situation every day. Given the current hostile, political climate, a more humane resolution is critical, yet pending. I live every day in constant confusion, anxious to find out what awaits me. In spite of the uncertainty, I choose to use those emotions as a source of strength and resilience. I will not yield to fear.

When I was eighteen years old, I went to a community retreat. I naïvely volunteered to answer a life-defining question: *What is the one thing that jumps to mind when you think about what you fear the most?* This innocent inquiry conjured a vivid memory of Immigration and Customs Enforcement ICE officials storming into my house in the middle of the night, pushing and shoving their way in. I was ten years old and with the little English I could speak, I asked them what they were looking for. They weren't looking for a thing; they were looking for a person. My dad.

My mom, who did not understand English, was standing next to me. I could feel her frustration and fright as if it were my own. In that instant, I became the spokesperson for my family. With my voice shaking, I told the officials my dad was not home. They ignored me and continued to rifle through the rooms, turning the beds over, assuming he was hiding. In a split second, I remembered something I had heard on the news and shaking in fear, I asked them for a signed warrant. They became visibly upset and were surprised a child would challenge them. Since they didn't have a warrant, they had no option but to leave.

At the community retreat in Philadelphia, in front of a room with approximately sixty strangers, I responded to the question honestly. I saw their shocked faces. Some nodded in agreement while others shook their head from side to side in disapproval of my story. At that moment, I did not think much of anyone's reaction. I was reflecting about what scared me the most and felt proud that I had emerged from the shadows at age eighteen. I was able to shed light on a situation that is a way of life for millions of people throughout the U.S.

At that time, I did not fully comprehend what it meant to be undocumented. I didn't quite understand the stigma associated with not being a citizen. I did not see my status as something that needed to be guarded or protected, much less kept a secret. I vividly recall when the attendees of the conference came up to me and strongly recommended, I never mention my citizenship status again in public. It was just not something to share, they said.

I felt perplexed. I didn't understand why complete strangers were advising me to remain in the shadows. At that moment, something from within emboldened me to speak up. I felt empowered and refused to become voiceless. I vowed to become an example for people experiencing a similar situation, just as others had inspired me. Among these inspiring individuals are my sister, Maria R. Gonzalez, a continuous advocate for immigrant rights. She is among many who broke barriers, navigated the challenges of attending college, obtained degrees, and now have fruitful careers in their respective fields. They, like myself, are proud contributors to the improvement of our communities.

LIFE IN FEAR

Twenty-three years ago, my family migrated to the land of opportunity, seeking a better life for their three children: Jose, age 15, Maria, age eight, and myself, only seven and a half. My parents risked crossing the desert with us in tow, not knowing what lay ahead for us at the end of the journey. As we embarked on crossing the border between Mexico and the U.S., the "coyote" helped protect me. He told me to pretend I was playing with my sister as we walked down a street that would lead us to the U.S. I wasn't fully aware of what was going on, but as I saw ICE officers guarding the area with guns and frowns, I immediately became scared. The officers scowled when their glare met my eyes, but they never said a word to us as we didn't appear suspicious. My family and I walked down the street to a McDonald's on the U.S. side to meet up with another coyote. This new coyote would take us to Chicago, our new home - where the start of our new journey would begin.

My mom left her home country of Mexico without knowing anyone in the U.S. She did something that scared her a lot, all for her family. As Latina professionals, we always discuss the value of taking risks. Most of our parents took the biggest risk of their lives so we would have the chance to do the same. My mom didn't hold back when thinking about her family's future. As I picture my parents crossing the border with their three children, I can't stop thinking about the words that give me strength, *"tú echale ganas, tú puedes, yo te apoyo."* (go for it, you can do it, I will support you all the way.) And those exact words push me to persevere when I am tired, because it is very tiring to live in uncertainty. My mother's words bring me comfort and compel me to start thinking about the things I *can* do; the things that I can change in my life and the positive impact I can create for others when sharing my story of success, despite the roadblocks.

While growing up in the U.S. and learning a new language, I was involved in extracurricular activities and went on to become a straight - A student. Once I started high school, I wanted to become more financially responsible, not only for myself but for my family. I began the process of getting a job. That was when my fear really set in and rose to the surface.

My reality was about to come to the forefront. I began to notice just how different I was. The life I lived was unique. My parents tried to explain to me that I couldn't get a job as easily as my other friends. I couldn't job hunt with my friends because I lacked the one thing that everyone needs to get a job—a social security number. I had no clue such a small piece of paper could carry so much weight.

I wondered what that really meant—to be undocumented. Little did I know that it meant that one hundred of the doors I knocked on would be closed before I even got there. Until that moment, I had not realized that I was undocumented. Once I started to understand the magnitude of my citizenship status, I understood that I had to fight not only twice, but three times as hard as anyone else. It wouldn't be easy to get where I wanted and be who I wanted to become.

MY VOICE ACROSS THE BORDERS

Over time, I realized that being undocumented meant restricted freedom. I was unable to attend my uncle's funeral in Mexico. He was someone very dear to my heart who saw me grow and raised me when I lived in Mexico. My mom was unable to go to her own mother's and father's funeral, even though my grandparents had taken us into their home and helped raise me and my two siblings. People of authority crushed my dreams before I could even attempt them.

During high school, my counselor scolded me for trying to apply to college. She strongly believed I would be rejected because of my citizenship status. When I mentioned to my mom that I wanted to go to college, she was honest.; *"Mija aunque no conozca este país y todo lo que se necesitas para ir al colegio, yo te apoyo. Tu puedes, echale ganas,"* she said. (Mija, although I don't know this country and everything you need to go to college, I will support you all the way, go for it, you can do it.) And those were the only words I needed to hear.

I didn't listen to those who attempted to oppress my choices or my growth. I applied to several universities and was accepted to them all. I obtained full ride scholarships for three of them, but didn't move forward with the acceptance because I was afraid that they would find out about my citizenship status and revoke the scholarships. Instead, I decided to enroll in a community college.

The lack of a social security number meant that I could not qualify for any financial aid or loans. Thus, community college was the most affordable option. As I started to look for guidance on how to obtain my undergraduate degree, I came across other people in similar situations. They too were undocumented and had managed to obtain their undergraduate degree. A few even had master's degrees. Hearing their success stories and learning that others like me were able to reach their goals inspired me to continue my long journey.

As I was looking to transfer to a four-year university, I had to manage two jobs while attending college. Although I wanted to follow the common four or five-year path to obtaining my undergraduate degree, this path easily became a seven-year journey. After finishing two years at a community college, I was forced to take a break in order to save enough to enroll in a university.

Continuing my professional development and growing my career involved facing more challenges. I continued working to save up for college but began to doubt myself. I was unsure if I should return to finish my degree. I kept on thinking, what will it matter? I wasn't going to be able to excel or grow in a career given my citizenship status. However, despite my own doubts, I kept on growing as a *mujer resistente, fuerte y con garra*. (Resilient woman, strong and empowered).

A year and a half later, I enrolled at the Illinois Institute of Technology (IIT), a private school that gave me a half-tuition scholarship. While enrolled at IIT, I completed my last two years of university and graduated with a B.S. in Business Administration. It was a busy and exhausting time in my life. My schedule consisted of going to class, rushing to my two jobs, and then commuting back to school. All of this was a daunting task to ask of someone so young, but I became a *mujer resistente*.

In 2012, President Obama announced his program for undocumented individuals who arrived at an early age in the U.S. and met certain requirements. It was called DACA (Deferred Action for Early Childhood Arrivals) and DACA gave me a status. I was able to obtain a job that required background checks, meaning higher pay. I suddenly became eligible to obtain a driver's license, a state ID, and travel without fear. I was given the opportunity to dream again. Additionally, I was able to take risks that would propel my personal and professional growth. I became one of over six million DACA recipients.

After obtaining DACA, I obtained a higher wage job to help pay my way through college. Most of the doors that were once closed suddenly opened for me. I no longer had to wonder what I would do with my degree. I didn't have to worry about walking down the street looking over my shoulder and panicking every time I heard a siren. I no longer had to worry that I would be the next ICE raid in my Chicago neighborhood of Little Village.

THE JOY OF DISCOMFORT

I continued to gain knowledge and develop as a professional. Navigating the business world as a DACA woman was not an easy journey. I continued to encourage and support other women while tending to my own personal growth. I joined a group called Latinas on the Plaza during my last semester in college. Through this program, I met many powerful women who inspired me to continue my career path and growth. Soon, I graduated from both Illinois Institute of Technology and Latinas on the Plaza, becoming the alumnae board chair of the program.

My role with Latinas on the Plaza and other life experiences gave me the courage to become comfortable making others uncomfortable when asking for what I deserve. I began to do things that scared me. I made the first move in asking for a promotion and negotiated a raise for myself. I left a job that wasn't making me happy, which was a hard decision because I needed it for my stability. Regardless, those were changes needed to achieve my ongoing success. I continued to be that *mujer poderosa, mujer resistente, mujer con garra.*

As I navigate through my career trajectory and am faced with new challenges, I keep in mind my mom's words *"tu echale ganas, tu puedes."* I continually ask myself, what am I scared of? I ask it when I want to go for a small challenge, like asking that guy for a coffee date or sending my resume to that multimillion corporate company. Why hold back?

I have overcome many unexpected obstacles. I continue to be vocal to empower other women and also get what I deserve rather than stay hidden and in the shadows. Although the initial fear I had at age ten and again at eighteen occasionally creeps up on me, I now use fear to empower me to keep growing. It now helps me continue to give my all and persevere in my endeavors.

As I continue to empower other women of color, I look back and see how far I have come. From leading committees at the young age of sixteen for Fiesta del Sol (the largest festival in the Midwest) to graduating from college and starting a career, I have worked my way up from administrative assistant to program coordinator and most recently program manager, managing programs for economic growth opportunities within the Latino community. I enjoy working in one of the highest revenue generating communities in Chicago, Little Village. Through my work with small businesses, I implement various programs that directly increase the revenue and visibility of local businesses.

Today, I am not only involved with organizations that offer career development resources and guidance, but I have become a mentor to other young women who seek career and personal development. Most recently, as the program manager for professional development programs at Hispanic Alliance for Career Enhancement (HACE). I provide a range of professionals with the tools necessary to thrive in their pursuits. Eager to create impact and to learn, I excelled in my position, encouraging high professional triumphs in high-potential Latinos and implementing processes for the program's success.

As I continue developing and growing, I want to remind every one of you that you are *mujeres poderosas, mujeres resistentes.* No matter what your background is, no matter the hardships, you have endured, do not allow yourself to plummet. Be proud of your background and embrace it fully. Once you embrace all the good and the bad, no one can stop your growth.

Don't let others silence or sway you from your goals. I know many times in our culture we are taught as women to be silent and humble, and speaking of our success is boastful and asking for what we deserve is being overambitious, and perhaps even pushy. We must rise from the shadows, be courageous in navigating our fears, gain strength and use that as a catalyst towards seeking what we deserve. Do not let anyone tell you that you are too ambitious, or unrealistic. You are a *mujer poderosa, mujer resistente, mujer con garra, mujer luchona, mujer entregada (powerful, resilient, empowered woman and warrior).* You get to be ambitious. You are entitled to want more because you have fought hard to thrive in the fruits of your hard labor.

Remember that you have traveled a long path to be where you are now, and you deserve to be there! If you are experiencing hardships, I want to encourage you to continue pursuing all of your dreams! Keep pushing because we are strong, resilient, and we have a voice.

Being undocumented is part of who I am; it has made me, powerful and persistent in accomplishing my goals. It has made me appreciate the opportunities that I have come across. It has made me a *mujer poderosa, mujer resistente, mujer guerrera.*

THINK YOUNG AND GROW

What are YOU most afraid of? Don't let it get in the way of using your voice.

You can't expect others to want to hear you. Go ahead and grab that seat at the table without asking for permission. Make your voice be heard. As women of color we face twice as many obstacles as other women. We must uplift our own voices and be loud! Start by removing those things that scare you from your life.

Try the following exercise:
1. Write down two or three things that drive you and make you get up in the morning at the very top of a piece of paper.
2. Skip a few lines, then add one thing which makes you feel out of your comfort zone. Do this every morning, for a week.
3. At the end of each day, make sure you have completed the one thing you wrote in the morning.
4. Hold yourself accountable by sharing this list with a close friend, sister, aunt, etc. and let them know you will accomplish all the things you wrote on that piece of paper by the end of the week.
5. Read this list every morning to remind you that you can shine and be a mujer poderosa. Remember this every time you do something out of your comfort zone.

THIS IS ME

I am Magdalena L. Gonzalez–Hernandez. After implementing various programs that directly increased the revenue and visibility of local Latino businesses, I have continued to empower professional women of color. In 2019 I graduated from the *Mujeres de HACE* program, which I also coordinated. Within eight months, I was promoted to a program manager role. I am currently the program manager for professional leadership programs at HACE. I continuously partner with program leadership to provide participants with the necessary tools to thrive and I support more than thirteen program cohorts across the nation. As a seasoned professional and lifelong learner, I am committed to continuous professional development.

💬 *I want to purchase my first home and become a property manager. I also dream of traveling the world and experiencing new cultures.*

THE FIVE-YEAR PLAN

1. Obtain my project management certification
2. Become part of the C-suite of a corporation
3. Launch my own makeup brand

GUERRERA DE MI VIDA

Sandra Lopez

"Stay true to yourself and have the courage to grow into who you really are, not who others think you should be."

There I was, ten years old and sitting in class when I heard my name called over the intercom. It was the school secretary informing my teacher that I needed to come down to the office because my mom was there. The rest of the students in the class started shouting comments like, "Aww... you're lucky, you get to go home early," or "Did your mom bring you McDonald's?" That's what usually happened when someone's parents came to school; they were going out to lunch or their mom or dad were bringing them McDonald's. But I knew that was not the reason my mom was here.

My mom would never pull me out of school to get McDonald's. Not my mom! She was the mom who drilled into my head how much I needed to go to school so that I could become someone in life. She would always remind me of what a privilege it was for me to go to school and receive a formal education. You see, my mother had emigrated from Mexico, alone, at the young age of twelve. She was the second eldest in her family of eight, but the eldest female and caretaker of her younger siblings. She was therefore not allowed to continue school beyond sixth grade.

As I gathered my things and walked down the hall, I felt an instant pit in my stomach. And then I saw my mother standing at the end of the hallway outside the school office. The look on her face told others nothing, but it told me everything. You see, despite my young age, I knew how to read my mother very well. Something was wrong. Once we got in the car, she started crying, and then began to tell me why she had pulled me out of school that morning. My little brother had suffered a seizure. I was only ten and wasn't entirely sure I knew what that meant, but I knew that in that moment it broke my mother's heart, so it broke mine too. Little did I know that was the day which would shape the rest of my life and the woman I would become.

A GUERRERA IS BORN

That day ignited a fire in my heart, and my champion spirit was born. I became more than my mother's translator; I became her rock. I would accompany her to my brother's doctor's visits, looking for answers about what was wrong with my brother. I helped her understand, despite the language barrier. Many would call this a tremendous responsibility for a ten-year-old, but I didn't mind at the time; I saw it as an opportunity to spend time with my mother and help her. I always saw my mother as a warrior, or what I call a *"guerrera,"* and because of this I wanted to be tough like her. This was my chance to be a *"guerrera,"* like her.

After countless doctor visits with different doctors, we finally received a diagnosis for my brother. The doctor said it was autism. You would think receiving a diagnosis would finally give my family the clarity we were seeking, but it didn't. We had no idea what the term autism meant, and we had never met anyone with autism. We felt lost, confused, and overwhelmed. The days following my brother's diagnosis, I spent a lot of time at the local library. That's where I would regularly walk to get help with school or spend time drawing, which I really enjoyed.

On one occasion I told the librarian what had happened with my brother, and she gave me books and a VHS tape on autism. This explained my brother's diagnosis better and helped me and my mother navigate his needs. Still, it was not enough. I knew that I needed to pursue a more formal education to demand the respect we deserved from doctors and ask the questions we needed to ask. Over the years it was difficult to maneuver the health care and school system with individual education plans (IEPs) and complex medical terminology. My mother did the best that she could with her basic English skills and the translation I could offer as a young girl. My mother and I often felt disrespected from the professionals in the field because of our lack of information and their lack of understanding and empathy towards immigrant families. We often left our doctor visits feeling deflated, confused, and frustrated.

CHANNELING MY INNER GUERRERA

I was born and raised in the northwest suburbs of Illinois. My parents emigrated from Mexico and divorced when I was a little girl. I grew up in a closely-knit family where siblings and cousins were as tight as they come. Early on, art became my therapy. It was my escape when things would get rough at school and home. I soon became the kid that always had a broken piece of crayon in my pocket and loved using sidewalk chalk every chance I got. I was a very adventurous little girl; I just didn't know it yet.

Growing up, I didn't have professional mentors. However, I come from a family of very strong women that always set the bar high for me. My mom has four sisters and I grew close to all of them. Although they might not have been my official mentors, I knew I needed to have their grit in life to accomplish my dreams.

I discovered my love for reading early on, and it soon became my gateway to my future. I found my professional mentors and guidance in books. I got the "ganas," (desire) from my family, but I was still not sure what I wanted to do in life or what I was capable of achieving.

My first official job was working at the coatroom at a local restaurant. It was the perfect job for me because I was able to read during my downtime, and I was able to talk and meet new people regularly. Those were two of my favorite things to do, but I never thought that my experience in the coatroom was the beginning of my career path. The conversations that I had with people in the coatroom were really what we would call networking today. Yet, the 15-year-old me didn't know it.

One day, a woman noticed that I liked to read, and she asked me if I ever considered working in a library. I remember thinking how this thought had never occurred to me. It was through this woman that I got my first library job and started working on a bookmobile. There I was able to combine my love for books and my passion for helping others. The bookmobile visited underserved neighborhoods primarily filled with immigrant communities. Because I spoke Spanish, I was able to help them connect with the resources they needed to improve their quality of life in the U.S. I felt very connected to the library patrons because I could relate well to their struggles and wanted to help in any way I could.

My brother's diagnosis forced us to grow as a family and as individuals. While still working at the library, I pursued a more formalized art education. My mother embarked on her journey of entrepreneurship and became a successful home business owner. This gave her more flexibility to attend to my brother's needs and offer more one-on-one care. It also allowed me more time to focus on school.

Some of my family and friends thought it would be a waste of time to pursue an art education. Sadly, I learned at a young age not to share my dreams and aspirations with people close to me because they often knocked me down and discouraged me. I would constantly hear comments from those closest to me like, *"Para que vas estudiar arte? Eso no sirve"* (What are you going to do if you study art?) *or "Te vas a morir de hambre...estudia algo que te de dinero como una doctora."* (You are going to starve ... study something that gives you money. Be a doctor!) In my family, if you were not following a traditional career path such as a doctor or a lawyer, then you were wasting your time. I remember my mother so desperately trying to make me change my mind about studying art that she told me she wasn't going to help me pay for school if I did. I knew my mother was not purposefully trying to hurt my feelings, but she did. It was her way of trying to guide me to a career with more job security.

But despite all the negativity from the people closest to me, and nobody believing in me or trusting in my potential, I used my intuition and tapped into my courageous heart to pursue what I wanted. I didn't know how I would do it, where I would go or where I would get the money, but I was going to study art. I knew I needed to make it happen, and I did.

The thought of not letting my brother down was in the back of my mind every step of the way. He needed me, but I knew I wasn't able to help him in any great capacity until I helped myself first. I applied to many great art schools and was accepted; some were public, and some were prestigious, private schools. I eventually selected Northeastern Illinois University because of its diversity and location. I was still able to drive back and forth to help my mom with my brother's needs whenever she needed me.

I enrolled myself and told my mom the news when I got home from work. First, she flipped out because not only did she disapprove of me studying art, she did not want me going to school in Chicago. In her mind, Chicago was dangerous and no place for a young Latina. She also didn't believe in moving out before marriage. She wanted to keep me safe and encouraged me to attend the local community college down the street. But I knew I couldn't because I was hungry for new experiences in my life and to discover who I really was. That required me to step out of my comfort zone.

GUERRERA IN THE CORPORATE WORLD

I left the library world to attend college full time and pursue my art education. Upon graduation, I got a job working for a Fortune 500 beer company. All of my friends and family told me how lucky I was to have the job and how they wished they could have a fun job like mine, working for a beer company. But despite finally getting my family's approval, I was miserable in the position. Yes, I had a stable income, health insurance, and abundant opportunity to grow with the company. I had the opportunity to travel out of the country for work and attend countless free concerts and games with great seats, but I was still miserable. I felt a void in my heart.

Then one night I came home from work and started sobbing uncontrollably, although I had not had a bad workday. I knew it was time to ask myself some hard questions. So, I decided to reflect and think back to the last time I was happy in life and felt truly fulfilled in my heart. I noticed a pattern in my life that kept repeating. I would leave the library world for other jobs or education, but I would always go back there, either to volunteer or work part time. I took this as a sign that I needed to go back to my calling, and this time, invest in it too. I resigned from my corporate job and decided to take the leap into the unknown with the hope that a safety net would appear.

Again, my family and friends thought I was nuts. I would hear comments like, "You're doing what? Why would you leave your job security? You want to leave beer for books? Why would you want to work for a nonprofit? You're stupid for leaving." But once again, despite all the negativity around me and lack of support, I pursued my heart's desire. I got a job as the community outreach manager for a library with a very diverse community and obtained my master's degree in library science from the University of Wisconsin-Milwaukee. It's a degree that only five percent of Latinas hold in the entire U.S. For the first time in my life, I looked back and felt proud of the woman I was becoming.

DEFENDER OF MANKIND

As the outreach manager for a library with a high immigrant population, I am an inclusion advocate for people of all abilities, including autism. I remember the challenges my family faced when I was growing up and our lack of access to information and acceptance from the community. As a manager for the library, I have become a voice for those who don't have one and because of this, new programs have been created. As a result, I have not just fostered awareness for autism, but acceptance of neurodiversity. Creating an environment where everyone is welcome has become my mission in my field and something I strive for every day.

We live in a world where empathy has to be taught, and I leverage my position at the library to spread that message. My library plans to someday host an accessibility hour in which the library will offer early entry one hour before the official open time to provide an inclusive, accommodating environment for families with special needs. In addition, bilingual (English & Spanish) caregiver and parent education, staff education, and sensory-friendly programming have all become a priority for the community.

When I asked my mom why she named me Sandra, she said because the meaning of my name is "defender of mankind." When I was a child, I thought that meant I had to defend the kids who were being bullied or be the protector of my siblings. But as I grew older, I realized that it's actually liberating to know that you can't protect everyone. Things happen. Life happens. Because of trauma, my family has grown closer and stronger. It is then that I also realized that while you can't protect everyone, you also can't please everyone. Follow your gut, make the most of every day, and be proud of who you are. I might not feel the need to be a superwoman anymore, but I have grown to be a true philanthropist at heart.

My driving force this whole time has been my brother. On all the hard days when I was growing up, feeling lost and wanting to give up because life was too hard or uncertain, I knew I couldn't because my brother was counting on me to become a champion in life. Despite being non-verbal, he has taught me some of the greatest lessons of my life. Most of all, he has given me the courage to discover who I am and what truly makes me happy. After all, courage doesn't mean you don't get afraid; it means you don't let fear stop you. At a young age, he became my why, my driving force behind every accomplishment I have achieved. He is a blessing and the glue that holds my family together when life throws us curve balls.

I have learned that sometimes those closest to you might not understand the choices you make or the journey you are on, but that's okay. Stay true to yourself and have the courage to grow into who you really are, not who others think you should be. In the end, those who matter will accept you and love you for who you are.

THINK YOUNG AND GROW

What have you lacked the courage to do in your life? I encourage you to take the time to reflect and identify the patterns in your life that will help you recognize the path of your destiny. As an exercise, create a timeline of your life using pen and paper. I invite you to be the captain of your own destiny and ride the waves your heart yearns for. Don't let fear stand in the way of living your dreams and aspirations and most importantly, learn to tune out other negative comments, including your own negative self-doubt. You have to be the one to rise to the occasion and trust the process; no one will do it for you.

THIS IS ME

My name is Sandra Lopez and I am a first-generation American who is proud of her Mexican culture. I am an outreach manager for a public library in the northwest suburbs of Illinois. I am an artist and owner of Cafeart studio and an advocate for the inclusion of those of all abilities. I received a BFA from Northeastern Illinois University and an MLS from The University of Wisconsin-Milwaukee. I am a defender of mankind.

To open up an art studio that embraces Latinx culture but is inclusive to all.

Stay true to yourself!

THE FIVE-YEAR PLAN

1. Open up a physical space for my art studio where those of all abilities are welcome and people can come together to collaborate on art projects and create a sense of community.
2. Travel to three new countries
3. Become a Reiki Master

Council to serve the local Fiesta del Sol as a member of the ground crew committee. I was scared, but it was one of the few ways I could make money at my age. I had some help from a mentor from my church named Katie, who attended the council meetings with me. Little did I know that my involvement would become life changing.

I was active with the festival and the council for ten years. I eventually chaired the ground crew, known as the Sol Team committee, and developed leadership and management skills that would someday help me in my career, even though I didn't yet know what that would be. I was responsible for interviewing, hiring, scheduling, and making a budget leading multiple teams that totaled 120 plus youth ranging from 14-19 years old. This experience helped me choose management as a future career path.

At Pilsen Neighbors, I found the right mentors and role models to steer me towards the path to higher education. After graduation, they helped me pursue & apply to colleges, navigate the application process and find financial aid. Because of my hard work chairing the Sol Team, I was able to receive the Guadalupe A. Reyes Scholarship for four years. I was so grateful to receive help for college, just for doing what I liked to do, and being part of an organization that helps one another and gives to those that need help as well. In the fall, I enrolled at Northeastern Illinois University. Four years later, I graduated with my bachelor's degree in Business Management with a minor in criminal justice. It made me the first person in my family to obtain a college degree and pave the way for my younger siblings and relatives to do the same.

SELF LOST

Who would have thought that something that you hear about on a TV show could actually happen to you? Four years ago, I was with a friend and coworker. We were walking back to my vehicle that was parked outside her house when we were suddenly attacked. Everything happened so fast, and it was so painful. I can only remember pieces of the event. Two males came out from some side bushes and grabbed hold of each of us. They asked us for our money, but we really didn't have much on us besides our wallets and cell phones. It was summer and I was traveling light.

At one point, my assailant pushed my friend onto my car, and it activated the alarm/sensor because we had the keys to the vehicle. Then they continued to shove us around on the ground and began to pull off our clothing. While all this was happening, I had various emotions roaring through me. I felt fear, helplessness, and a sense of surrender. I recall getting hit across my face, then falling to the ground only to be able to see my friend across from me with another man on top of her. I squirmed with my own assailant on top of me, desperately trying to get free. All these emotions had me in some sort of shock-state, something I can't really explain. I didn't know what was going to happen to us and I felt like my body just gave out. The assault got physical, but at one point they were able to get hold of the car keys. They struggled a bit to get into the vehicle, but when they did, they quickly drove off and left us in the middle of the street.

My friend reacted quickly and pulled me away from

the oncoming car. So many things happened that night that I couldn't understand or cope with any of them. How did this happen to me? To us? I was always careful, or at least I thought I was. I did not feel I deserved to have this happen to me. The police report said I was the victim of an assault and vehicular hijacking. The way I explain the crime is to ask others if they've ever watched an episode of Law & Order SVU. In the show, the crime happens, victims get medical attention, and the police gets involved to investigate. In real life, crimes don't get resolved in 60 minutes. It takes days, weeks, months, even years to get some sort of resolution.

I was now a VICTIM, something I never in my life thought I would ever be. Being a victim of a crime was all new to me and I was traumatized. First, all I did was cry it out for days, even weeks. I had so many mixed emotions and I no longer felt strong. I felt like I was not Cristina anymore. I felt like I did not know myself, like I had lost something integral to my being. Or so I thought.

Right after the attack, I was taken to the hospital where I was given many tests and medication. As all this was happening, I remember that all I wanted was my mother. I needed someone who was always there for me, someone to make things better. The pain and the feeling of being lost just wasn't sinking in. I started thinking about my job and how I had to tell them I would not be in. I was able to reach my employer and within a few hours, my family was also with me at the hospital. At that moment, all I needed was my mom to hug me tight and not let me go. Her hugs would make me feel safe, or at least that's what I thought. My hope was that with her hug, the pain I was feeling would just vanish. Obviously, that wasn't so, but wrapped in her arms, I felt it was all within reach. I felt so disgusted with myself; how could I have let this happen?

After the hospital, I was taken back to my mother's house where I laid on her living room couch. Soon, detectives were at the door, looking to speak to me. Once you've been involved in a crime, there is no rest or regard for your time or space. I now understand why this is so. The detectives needed as many details about the incident as possible, and anything else I could tell them to further their investigation. Within a few hours, the detectives located the vehicle. A week later, they caught the assailants.

SELF RESTORED

I immediately returned to work the next day after the accident, but I was still in shock. There were times I felt uneasy around a certain group of people, but the only thing I knew to do was to get back to my regular routine, which meant returning to work. Even though I wasn't feeling one hundred percent strong, I tried to appear as if nothing had happened. But as soon as I got home and was alone, I would feel shame for putting myself in that predicament. I thought about how this criminal act would change me, my friend, and the assailants. I should have known better. I was worried about what everyone would say about me and how everyone would even look at me from then on. I was fearful of pursuing the case and facing retaliation. I even thought about how putting the assailants in jail would change their lives if I did that.

I struggled so much with my decision to prosecute them, even though I knew what I had to do. We needed to get justice but at the same time, I could not process it. I'm glad I reached out for help because it's hard to think clearly when you are in a traumatic, emotional state. Dealing with the assault has been the biggest challenge in my life, and the most difficult to overcome mentally and emotionally. I've done everything I could do to heal. I've pursued the crime, seen a therapist who offered an unbiased viewpoint and helped me sort out and talk about my feelings and been there for my friend, who was also suffering, too. Together, we participated in lineups to point out our assailants, attended court hearings, and soon it came down to the option of a plea bargain.

Every step of the way was frightening, but deep inside, I knew it was the right thing to do. Because I had some knowledge of the criminal/justice system from school, I was able to stand my ground and fight the injustice done to me and my friend. I accepted full responsibility for the actions going forth in order to get justice. I decided I had not come so far in my life to be taken down by this event.

While all this was happening, I was participating in a class to be promoted within my company and struggled with finishing it. I wanted to quit. I had too much on my plate with being a victim and trying to find myself for my own emotional survival. But at the same time, I only had one more class and I was done.

I just had to present the project I had been working on for four months prior to the incident. I asked my friends and my therapist what to do, and they all advised me to finish. One friend said to me, "What can you really lose, versus what you can actually gain from finishing the class?" These words pushed me to put on my presentation mindset and do it. As much as I thought I wasn't going to do well, I proved to myself that I could. I passed and was promoted. Everything I had worked for from my education, to my career development, had paid off. Who said a tragic event would hold me back? I am the only one who will define my outcomes.

SELF ASSURED

I love the words of Frida Kahlo, "al fin del dia, podemos soportar mucho más de lo que creemos que podemos" which translates into "at the end of the day, we can endure much more than we think we can." I illustrate this sentiment, because I have dealt with so much more than I ever thought I could. The support from my family, friends, and from my own self has given me the strength to share my experience with those who can relate to the same feelings I have had.

Looking back at that moment in my life, I can't believe I survived and overcame it. But I did! Now, even more than before I believe anyone can overcome anything and everything. Sure, things are tough but with some help and understanding we can pick ourselves back up and continue. I know that we shouldn't give up and that we should actually ask for help and consider all alternatives other than the easy way out. It can be a challenge of course, but in the end, it is all worth it. There is a light at the end of the tunnel. I was able to find myself and regain the strength to be able to get back on track with my life, and live life without fear holding me back. I do admit that traumatic events change you, but you decide which way it will define you.

With time, I was able to cope and make it through the minefield. With time, I was able to develop, find help and fight to achieve the success I can share with others.

Always keep in mind that you should do what you love to do. That's ultimately what will keep you going. I am now part of the Fuerte program, a woman's organization focused on empowering women for growth and development. I can honestly say that by becoming a member of the Fuerte program, I am once again experiencing the same joy I did when I was involved with organizations that can help others.

I want my story to show others that no one is alone in those times of need and darkness. We all reach these tipping points and we need to believe we can overcome them. We must find a way to come out of those moments of depression and despair and say, "WE GOT THIS!" and believe that anything is possible if we just keep going. If you feel lost, ask someone for help, but don't give up!

THINK YOUNG AND GROW

Have you ever been too hard on yourself? I've been there, done that, and know. I can attest to the fact that it can seem difficult to see some of the positives during tough times, but we cannot keep digging ourselves a hole to crawl into every time we get scared. We must raise ourselves up, stand up with our heads held high, and show that we are resilient at all costs. We have all come a long way and have even longer to go.

I challenge you to write down your many accomplishments. Ask those close to you to help you build your own book of praises. Then use the praises as "pick-me-ups" in those tough times when you doubt yourself, have had a bad day, or failed a project. Let the book motivate you to keep going and be your support. The book will remind you that you've made "boss moves" and you can continue moving forward, even when times get hard, because you already have!

THIS IS ME

My name is Cristina Ramirez. I'm a first-generation college graduate from Northeastern Illinois University. I am currently in a traveling phase, visiting various states through work trips and on my own time to experience different scenery and cultures. I love my family and will continue to be a role model to my younger siblings, nieces, and nephews. I want to let them know that anything and everything is possible. We must just reach for our dreams!

My dream is to travel to Paris and continue traveling all over the world.

THE FIVE-YEAR PLAN

1. Acquire real estate that I can call my own home
2. Have my own personal library at home
3. Become a motivational speaker

BEYOND

Aline Lamadrid

"Loving yourself is the answer."

"Hey! What's my name?" I've asked people, wondering how they'll reply. Their answer is usually a look of bewilderment and confusion. They wonder why I don't know my own name. So I get more specific.

"No, I mean, how would you say my name?"

A pause.

Then their response is usually something along the lines of *EI-LEEN or AI-LEEN*, which is not surprising since I've always introduced myself as the latter.

The more I thought about it, the more perplexed I became about my name. For a long time, I disliked my name. I hated the way it sounded on other people's tongues. I hated the look of confusion it garnered upon seeing how it was spelled. I longed to be named something else, something simpler. Over time, though, I learned to love the uniqueness of my name.

Aline. It's pronounced…

AH-LEE-NEH.

My very first birthday gift. Why is it that I had twisted something so beautiful and changed it into EI-LEEN? Eileen is also a very beautiful name, it's just not my name. When did I begin to change the pronunciation of my name, and for whose convenience?

When I tell them the pronunciation, they're confused.

"Wait... I say your name as UH-LEEN..."

CRUEL NEW WORLD

My parents brought me to the U.S. at the age of seven, so there's not much I remember about arriving except the unforgettable first breath of the cold winter air. The chilly night marked a new beginning. The dark sky felt overwhelming, there were countless lights surrounding me, and in the vast sea of artificial lights, it felt as if I was the only lonely shining star blinking in the sky, blind to the galaxy laid before my eyes.

I began first grade without an ounce of English in me. When the teacher asked me to introduce myself, I confidently responded, "Aline." That confidence dwindled as my time in school progressed.

There were a lot of things that I couldn't control. I couldn't control the fact that I was in the U.S., and I couldn't control that when the whole class began to sing in English, I was utterly lost and began to cry in desolation. I couldn't control that whenever my classmates did activities that asked where they were born, I never knew how to respond because I feared that I would be seen as different from the others. So, I clung to the known and to what I could control; I worked and studied and within a year, they transitioned me into regular English classes and out of English Language Learners (ELL).

I never had the chance to grow up like other kids. I didn't have to worry about sports or music lessons or anything like that because it was an expense we couldn't afford, especially when it required my parents to drive me to and from places. Despite not having everything everyone else did, I never once blamed them; my parents always tried to provide us with everything we needed, even if it was not everything we wanted.

The first time we moved was into our first apartment during the middle of my fifth-grade year. We finally had a place to call home. Sure, the place was very small. But it was ours.

Education became a prime focus for me. I spent hours reading books, most of which were fantasy books with protagonists that I longed to emulate. I wanted to be fearless and confident, because confidence was a major struggle for me, especially during middle school.

As a young girl, I remember feeling hurt and insecure from the comments people threw me about my weight or how much I ate. I remember jokes I didn't find funny. The nicknames they came up with were hurtful and scarring. I wished to be someone else. I wanted to have blonde curly hair, bright blue eyes, and somehow feel prettier.

The summer before eighth grade, the darkness and negativity overtook me. During summer vacation, I stayed hours at home alone. All those comments from others came back to haunt me.

In my head, I heard the voice of a guy calling me fatty every time I overate. I relived the mockery and insults. I loathed my body and myself.

Pretty soon, it became almost impossible to have a full stomach without throwing up. It was a nasty habit, and my body became addicted. I knew that what I was doing was very wrong, so I hid it as best as I could. I felt that if I told my parents they would laugh or ridicule me. I felt gross and lost. I just wanted to be okay. Everything that I did was wrong, and I regret not seeking help or talking to my parents sooner.

Then, during the middle of eight grade, we had to move again, and I was the new girl once more. I always hoped to become someone outgoing, but most of the time I felt as if I was hiding in someone's shadow. So, with my heart in my hand, I began trying to make new friends. I met a lot of friendly faces, but still missed my best friend. I will forever be grateful to everyone who showed me kindness and understanding.

I wanted to live life to the fullest. I wanted to be me, to be free. But freedom isn't really free. I wanted to become a better version of myself, one who loves me. I began to put myself in uncomfortable clothing to try to become more confident, more accepting of myself. It never helped, because I never felt pretty enough. It's been a long journey, but as I discover who I am, I find myself with more confidence and certainty.

It wasn't until my sophomore year of high school that I completely stopped binging and purging. Eating disorders are serious problems that can affect anyone. There is so much social pressure to look or be a certain way that it becomes suffocating and it seems like there's no other way out. For a middle school girl to feel that way is not okay. Telling a middle school girl still undergoing puberty that it's not okay to eat with pleasure is wrong. It's important to encourage children to eat healthy, but healthy doesn't mean starving, healthy doesn't mean skinny, and skinny doesn't mean happy. In our community, it's important that these issues are taken seriously and that they're not thrown to the side and labeled as *"exagera,"* (exaggeration) because that keeps us from reaching out to the people we love and trust the most.

 In high school I noticed that I wasn't the same person that I was in middle school. I became more outgoing and outspoken. I'm very grateful for all the lessons that I learned from others. Sometimes the people I considered close to me ended up leaving me because of one thing or another. Each friend I lost brought me pain, because I opened my heart and I was vulnerable, and I was left wondering what was wrong with me. This continued on throughout high school. I cried for an answer; what was wrong with me? What could I do to stop them from leaving?

 It's not easy loving yourself and it's not easy feeling like an outcast. There are many times when I feel like I don't belong anywhere. The United States of America is a beautiful place. But I long for fresh air, for that feeling of belonging. I'm stuck in the land of the free, without freedom. I'm in a weird place where I'm too American to be Mexican, yet I'm too Mexican to be American, here in a country that treats me like an outcast, that proves that dreams come true, only sometimes, only if you have something more. I do love you, America.

Yet I'm homesick.

I miss my Grandma.

I'm disoriented.

Where is my home?

I don't know any place other than you, America; why can't I go discover? I wish to grow wings one day. I dream that this pain I'm feeling now is only the momentary pain and sores of sprouting wings. When my wings sprout, I will fly; wings are made to fly. For now, all I can do is run. I may never be able to reach the sky; I may never sprout those wings, but if I can help push someone off the cliff to begin their flight, that is what I'll continue to do.

Why me?

It has to be me. God has chosen this path for me because He believes I'm strong enough to overcome it.

It has to be me.

I remember crying like a baby, letting out all of my frustration at the Secretary of State's office. I had tried to get my license, and once again, I was rejected. Apparently, the documents I had weren't valid, even though I had already asked about them before. My efforts were ignored and with tears running down my face, I was asked to step aside. I walked out of the office, my tears blinding me as I tried hard to contain my sobs. The chilly air hit me. When will this winter end, I thought?

I had eagerly awaited my eighteenth birthday to finally have a license. I counted the days, made sure I had everything I needed, and now I was back to square one.

I turned right.

And I cried.

I cried because living was so hard, because breathing felt so hard. I cried because nothing seemed to go right and because despite all my efforts, it felt like I was going nowhere.

I just want to be normal. I just want to be normal. I repeated this like a mantra in my head.

I just want to take it easy; why must everything be so hard? I hoped my tears rinsed the wounds in my heart, but the salt in my tears made my heart ache even more deeply. I wept for the things I wanted but could never have, for a place to belong, for someone to tell me that I will accomplish all my dreams, that this was just a speed bump. As my sorrow came to a slow halt, I quickly tried to look as normal as possible. I wiped my tears away and looked into my camera to see my puffy eyes staring back at me. My parents were picking me up soon and the last thing I wanted was for them to feel guilty or sad. I wouldn't be the person I am today without them.

So, I picked myself up and walked around. *"Bring the pain on,* sang the music in my headphones. Anger and power filled me. Yes, things seemed rather bleak at the moment, but the rain doesn't last forever, and winter lasts just for a season. I have to keep fighting, I have to break through and show myself that I'm the strongest person. That I've done it.

It's really frustrating feeling helpless with that sensation of not having control.

Sometimes I see so many people rushing around. I see

people working hard and being successful and yet I'm still here. Why do I feel like I'm running a marathon but I'm the only one running in place? Everyone gets ahead, everyone knows exactly where they're going, yet I push and run harder and breathe harder. Still, no matter how much air goes into my lungs, it never seems to be enough.

MY WINGS, MY GALAXIES

In time, in bits and pieces, I've come to realize that people walk in and out on their own, relationships are mutual, and there really is no use in changing yourself to please others. It's scary to be vulnerable, yet it's necessary.

I've found encouragement from seven young men that I greatly admire. The Bangtan Boys (BTS) helped my journey towards self-love and growth. They're one of my biggest inspirations: seven Korean men whose passion is palpable, who speak with their heart and have managed to reach millions, regardless of race, ethnicity, or language. Listening to their music filled me with inspiration and made me reflect on myself and my feelings.

They've taught me that my dream doesn't have to be something glamorous; if my dream is to breathe just for another day, then that's just fine. They've encouraged me to use my voice and speak my story, to keep running even if it feels like I'll never fly; that other opinions of me shouldn't matter as long as I know who I am. Through the simple things, through the hard times, everything can be fine.

My other inspiration is my parents. They were teenagers when I came into their lives. It fills me with awe whenever I see how far they've come when they tell me their stories. To my dad, who puts his life on the line every single day washing skyscraper windows to bring food to the table, and my mom, who raised us to be kind and compassionate, I can't express the amount of gratitude I have for them, as well as the countless other Latino moms and dads who do so much for their kids. You are my biggest heroes.

I've had many people who support me. I wouldn't be here if it weren't for them. My eyes have opened a bit more, and I sometimes wish to weep for the sorrows of the world and hope that it's enough to ease the world from suffering. It's very true that the standards we set for ourselves are much higher than the standards we set for others. I've come to realize that loving yourself is the answer. I've heard the expression, "You can't love others if you don't love yourself." However, I think differently.

You can love someone before you love yourself. You can love them more than you'll ever love yourself. However, the more you love yourself, the more you'll see clearly the amount of love you truly deserve to receive from others; that's why self-love is important.

I've spent a lot of my time hating myself, wishing to be someone else and criticizing every aspect of myself. Now, the legs that I once hated for making me too tall are legs that I cherish for taking me to many beautiful places; the eyes I once wished to be a lighter color are now eyes that I love for granting me the magic of seeing the people I love every single day; the stomach that I once loathed for being too "bulgy," I appreciate for digesting the food my mother makes with so much love.

I've also come to realize my achievements are greater than I think. My achievements are valuable, and they're not any less than anyone else's. Looking back to the time when I couldn't formulate a sentence in English, I feel proud of how far I have come, and how I am now someone I want to be.

There are times where the anger over injustices become overwhelming. The majority of my AP classes lack diversity and those classes are where I feel like I'm not me. Aline becomes a quiet character, someone who doesn't speak up, who's afraid to ask questions and feels inferior. It fills me with rage, watching myself be excluded from group activities because my classmates don't make the effort to include me and I don't make the effort to speak up. I'm not ashamed of who I am; I love every part of my race, culture, and background. I once thought that I was a boring person. But it was lie I told myself to convince myself that I was the same as everyone else.

I'm not.

We all have different stories. I'm not Earth, or Mars; I am not the Sun either. I am the Milky Way. I am the galaxy filled with billions of stars and stories, filled with dreams and scars. My worth isn't determined by anyone else; my worth is my own. I deserve to be respected, to be independent, and to be unapologetically me. Mentally stuffing the contents of my galaxy into the tight mold of a small planet changed me into something

I couldn't recognize. There were many moments in which I desperately wanted to believe that my self-worth amounted to nothing, that I was never going to be able to achieve anything, that I should just live a comfortable life. Yet I kept waking up in the morning to a new day, a new experience with brand new eyes, something I always want to do because you never know when your ordinary life will turn into something extraordinary.

I've learned to explore the contents of my own galaxy and the preciousness within them. There are many things about myself that I've yet to learn, and some which I practice to change, but the me with all my scars and mistakes is a me that has learned and morphed into a new star in the constellation of my galaxy.

Each person in the world is their own galaxy, each with different stars and planets, and I hope the day can come where our galaxies intersect and embark upon a journey of growth and happiness, where we explore the countless possibilities beyond.

I wish to wake up one day and smile at the me from today and tell her that her wings have sprouted. I wish to tell that seven-year-old girl that no matter how dark that sky may look, no matter how lonely you seem to be, you're not alone. Billions of stars and galaxies are hidden in the darkness beyond your eyes. Don't be afraid, because you don't shine alone, and one day, you you will meet and learn the stories of those constellations.

As the great Kim Namjoon from BTS says, "No matter who you are, where you're from, your skin color, your gender identity, just speak yourself. Find your name and find your voice by speaking yourself."

My name is Aline Lamadrid, what is your name?

THINK YOUNG AND GROW

Look at yourself in the mirror.

Explore your face in a new light. Give yourself a compliment, something you haven't thought of before. Tell yourself your name. Remind yourself of who you, and most importantly, remind yourself that you will get through anything. Believe in yourself. Every aspect of you was crafted into perfect imperfection, into a beautiful wreck. Embrace that.

Jamais Vu is the feeling of unfamiliarity despite seeing something constantly. That is life. Every day may seem the same, but live each day with curiosity, because every day is different. The greys and shadows in your life are needed to add definition to your life, to make the vibrant colors stand out. Look at yourself in the mirror and become your biggest fan. Love yourself like there's no tomorrow, because tomorrow, a new day will begin.

THIS IS ME

My name is Aline Lamadrid and I'm a first-generation student who will soon begin college in the fall of 2020, most likely in state. I hope to one day travel and gain perspectives and ideas in ways I can help others.

My dream for the future is to encourage and inspire others through my words and actions.

THE FIVE-YEAR PLAN

1. Graduate college
2. Travel out of the country
3. Give my Grandma a hug

"¿NENA, OTRO NOVIO?"
(GURL... ANOTHA MAN?!)

Marisol "Pinqy Ring" Velez

"There's no love like self-love."

I'm sitting on this couch I know too well, running my fingers across the green cloth as I trace its pattern with my stiletto nails. I've been here so many times, you would think that I live in this space. I know every corner and crevice, recalling memories of both happiness and hurt. Breakthroughs and barriers. Laughs and wailing cries. I breathe deeply—in through the nose, out through the mouth. My anxiety makes my legs quake in my gold and black Timbs, and my mind is running around itself trying to desperately control this situation.

This is my safe space.

This person loves me, and they could never leave me.

There is obviously some sort of mistake.

That becomes my mantra.

Then, I hear the dreadful words drip out. "I cannot see you any longer."

My heart stops... but not enough to mean that I'm dead. Just enough to know this is a pain that's going to make a home in my chest for a while.

I mean, I've done this before. I've felt this panging pain, I've battled for love and lost, I've been dark and left without the person I thought would light my life forever. I've done this before.

But... How do you deal with a breakup, again?

I'm not talking about a breakup with a partner, either. I'm talking about a breakup with my therapist. But, let's be honest - my relationship with men has definitely contributed to the reason that I sat in her office weekly for years on end.

I've always said that my breakup letters were like literary masterpieces. They could be framed in a museum on the intersection of Lost and Finding Myself. As a young girl who was told what to believe, who to be, how to dress and not to speak, it was hard to advocate for myself and say out loud what my feelings were. So, I wrote them out, attacking partners for leaving, attaching myself to the next man who would love me—even if only for a moment. I was an empty shell of unrequited love, trying to find myself through these losses, until I finally had to face the (wo)man in the mirror.

"¿NENA, QUIEN TU ERES?" (GURL... WHO ARE YOU?)

When I was a little girl, they would call me *Fosforito*. It means "little matchstick," and as a red-headed, freckle-faced Puerto Rican girl, I was literally a matchstick. A fervent fire never wanting to be tamed. I was a blaze; spunky, intelligent, adventurous, kind, talented, and funny as hell. Picture me, sassy-mouth lil' Spanglish-speaking Chicago girl with fire-colored hair looking like the Puerto Rican Pippi Longstocking. I was a unicorn from Chicago, a phoenix who would be reborn from the fire to truly find who she is.

I didn't always see myself in that positive light, however. For the longest time I didn't have a kind word for myself. As a *nena* who was brought up in a restricted and religious household, raised by watchful eyes that didn't let me self-actualize, I had no idea how to even begin figuring out who I was. I identified only with my pain, like it was my last name. As a survivor of childhood sexual abuse by two men in the church, my life changed before I could even understand how the consequences of someone else's actions would impact me. All the positive things about that spunky, fiery, and funny girl fell by the wayside and I became an angry teen, acting out and seeking any way possible to fill voids and veil trauma.

Enter: Men. *Nena*, this subject could be a book of its own! I could write for days about all the dudes who've burrowed themselves in and out of my life. It took a while to realize I would have to learn the hard lessons tucked in their arms. As I re-read my poetic letting go letters, there is so much pain. They were rehashing my traumas without even knowing it—there were proclamations of my selfless and unconditional love, there were questions that would forever go unanswered, there was blame for things only I could control.

Let's not get it twisted—my exes were definitely trash. I

could never excuse some of the pain these men put me through. But I wish I had known how to turn on the self-love switch and disconnect my heart from them much, much sooner. For so long, my identity was placed in the hands of those who I loved and those who (I thought) loved me. I didn't find myself until I painfully separated my soul from theirs and quickly found another man to melt into.

In those letters, however, I also see strength. There was so much power in advocating for myself, little by little, and championing for the kind of love I knew I deserved. So instead of focusing on the novios, I want to talk about how putting myself first (finally!) and truly understanding who I am led to the most revolutionary love I've ever felt.

"¿NENA, CUANDO TE VAS A DESPERTAR?"
(GURL, YOU WOKE. SO WAKE UP!)

Music and writing were how I found myself. Hip Hop was my therapist before I even knew about mental health, and definitely before it became a thing that we could talk about without shame. I consider my truest self as asleep until music finally woke me up. It was a wonder to me how Hip Hop could weave words into stories that I identified with. How it could talk about 'hoods and humanity over head-bobbing beats. I couldn't actually listen to rap music because of my parent's religion, so it became sort of my rebellion. I would sneak onto the computer for nights on end, downloading songs to listen to them in my Geo Prizm, learning and jotting down the emcee's prophetic lines.

(Yes - we couldn't just look up lyrics online.) It's no wonder, then, that when I picked up a pen and started writing my own truths to rap music that my very Puerto Rican parents would be incredibly confused that I wanted to make a career out of it. I had to go through a fire to find myself, and for them to accept the version of me I was becoming.

In 2004 my life would change forever. I woke up in Chicago's Cook County hospital, glaring lights beaming into my eyes, completely perplexed as to where I was and why. When I finally realized I was in a hospital, I panicked, cursed every nurse out (remember that angry teen I was telling you about?), and tried to take out my IV to leave. I pivoted my legs around the bed to exit, and then... I fell. The nurses helped me off the floor (bless their souls, they go through so much!), and brought a mirror to my face. I had been in a car accident. Our car had hit another car head-on, wrapped around a pole, and burst into flames. Off-duty officers had rescued us from the wreck. I had just woken up from a coma, with broken teeth, a contusion on my brain, a cracked open head with stitches, and no business trying to escape.

Some people can't pinpoint the moment in their life that shifts their whole world, and though mine seems like a sad story, it really is one of triumph. Fosforito arose from the fire, and slowly began to make the necessary changes to truly love herself.

I went to my first therapy session at 27 years old. The therapist was someone I didn't like very much, a student who seemed very much uninterested in my ramblings and would often look out of the window when I spoke. She was the quintessential horror story of going to therapy, but I learned a lot from her. I would have so many important *cosas* to share about myself, but somehow a boy got in the way and we would focus on him instead. The same way I went through a myriad of *novios*, I went through *un monton* (a lot!) of therapists. Some I loved with all of me, some I could just barely stand, but just like my exes, they each played a role in reassembling me piece by piece until I finally felt whole. Until I finally woke up.

"NENA, TE AMO INFINITAMENTE"
(GURL, YOU ARE SO LOVED)

I recently dealt with another rough therapist breakup. I have dealt with so many of them that I would just throw my hands in the air and *rendirme* (surrender). Just like love, it was easier to quit. It was easier to believe it was not meant to be; it was not for me. I would literally tell myself that I'm the only person on earth who doesn't deserve adoration and would never receive love as beautifully as I give it.

As I was scrolling through Instagram, I saw a meme:

Negative Thought:

I believed it so deeply, it became true.

Positive Thought:

I believed it so deeply, it became true.

I felt immediately attacked. (And, while we're talking about Instagram: Gurl, when you gon' put that phone down and stop wasting time? We're only seeing snippets of complicated people's lives. It's not real, this moment - right now, right here - is what matters. *No lo olvides*—don't forget it.)

I felt attacked because it was telling me what I needed to hear. How many times have falsities become our truth? How many times have people, parents, or partners said things about us that became the cornerstone of our identities? How often do we have so many kind words and thoughts to give others while we pick through the scraps? How many times do we love someone more than ourselves, or allow our identities to become wrapped up in another being? How many more times will you give everyone but yourself a bit of grace?

And, trust me, this is coming from an expert on the matter. I still harm myself; I still find myself over-loving. I still get in my head and doubt my own magic. I still scroll through Instagram when I should be writing raps, or stories, or meditating, or making healthy meals. I still love people even though all the warning signs say they aren't good for me. I could give myself a chancletazo for how many times I neglect myself. But, don't we all? Change is a process—nena, it's a LONG one—and we have so much generational trauma to undo. But then, I think of my mother. My grandmother. My aunt, my sister, my circle of women and all the young girls I teach or reach through my music. We all have the strength of a tribe, and we are the radical soldiers of unconditional love that our ancestors dreamed about.

But we *have* to learn to love ourselves and allow ourselves to be loved in the process. Self-care is more than tea light candles and crystals. It's more than splurging and shopping and massages. It's sitting with your thoughts and re-programming them. It's *making mistakes*... so many mistakes. It's pushing yourself even when you don't think you can take a step further. It's realizing that it's you that has been in your way the whole time. It's witnessing the darkest parts of our lives and still adoring ourselves. 'Cuz, who else is going to do it? Nobody will ever love you like you do. No one possibly can. So put on your cape, *nena*, because it's time you step into and stand in your power. *Te lo mereces* - You deserve it.

I am so happy to say, I found love again. I sit in this room, on a beige couch with bright blue accent pillows, and we laugh. We cry. We hug hard. She has told me how much I—her patient—shifts the energy in a room and makes her day exponentially better. She looks forward to seeing me, she brags about me, she thinks that me being a rapper is super cool and she affirms me when I need it most. Maybe she won't be around forever, and that's okay. I have learned to enjoy her—and people, in general—just for today.

I am *Fosforito*, a fire - and so are you! We deserve all of the good things coming our way, but please don't forget to love yourself. Don't forget to give yourself grace, don't forget to take your time, and don't forget to give and receive happiness *porque nena* - YOU ARE SO LOVED.

THINK YOUNG AND GROW

We all need some good words to live by. Here are some things that I learned from changing therapists, (and changing *novios*) that I hope can help you.

- Some things just don't last forever. And, that's okay.
- We literally can only control ourselves and our own reactions.

- Some people are terrible. Some people are fantastic. But they are all just humans with their own baggage, trying to figure it all out.
- Letting go is a process, and it gets easier with practice.
- Opening up and being vulnerable is really gangsta, even if it doesn't turn out how you expected.
- Change gon' come. And, that's also okay.

THIS IS ME

My journey through life (and mental health), came from simply trying. Trying different medications until the right one balanced me. Trying different therapists that I either hated or loved so much that it tore me apart when they had to go. Trying to follow my heart. Trying to love myself, even when it was really, really hard. But as I sit here in my new, two-bedroom apartment, (which will soon become my business hub and recording studio), I am just in awe of the way my life turned out.

I became the first in my family to graduate from college, with honors. I've won grants from the City of Chicago to rap, record, and tour. I teach a Hip-Hop class at a high school in my beloved Puerto Rican community of Humboldt Park. I became a U.S. Hip Hop Cultural Ambassador, traveling to Cambodia and Morocco under the flag of Hip-Hop diplomacy. I was recently hired as a site manager for this incredible program and will be flying to Nepal and Sri Lanka in the next year, (COVID permitting), to collaborate and facilitate international Hip Hop exchanges. Independently, I travel and perform and speak in different cities, universities, schools and nonprofits across the world, witnessing some of the most amazing and resilient humans I've ever met.

And now, I am writing an excerpt for a book to inspire young Latinas (and women, in general) just like myself! I thank my family, mentors, spirit guides, therapists, friends, and even those men who left me. Because I now realize I am a force to be reckoned with, a fire, and they all played a role in molding me. I look forward to seeing what's in store, but I now know the world is my (pink) oyster. I will continue to self-actualize in order to become an example of the transformative nature (and incredible power) of self-love.

To live in a world that is equitable for women, youth, people of color and my city - Chicago. For people to find their truths and live in them, unapologetically. Manifest a few boyfriends, too.

THE FIVE-YEAR PLAN

1. Continue to grow my Hip Hop music business in order to further my social impact and help women in music all over the world.
2. Travel to at least 5 new countries, sharing my story and encouraging folks to abolish imposter syndrome and find self-love.
3. Manifest infinite wealth and happiness for myself (and my community).

FEAR: I LOVE YOU, I HATE YOU, BUT OVERALL, I THANK YOU

Janine Arriola

"Faith replaced fear."

Roll on, you Blackhawks roll, roll on, you Blackhawks roll! The West Aurora High School fight song lingers in my mind. The memories and experiences that shaped my path rush back to me, as I sit and write about Fear. Yes, Fear. I operate from Fear, who is like an ever-present frenemy in my life. Let me explain how a four-letter word holds so much power. Even as I write this, Fear, and her sidekick, Anxiety, runs through my body; my mind fills with doubt, judgment, and excuses. Fear is the one who made me quit everything I ever started: karate, playing the organ, ballet, choir, volleyball, track…you get the picture. However, while my marriage with Fear is until death do us part, it is an emotion I have learned to allow myself to feel and overcome. It's ironic to say that Fear led me to join the military, because who joins the military because of Fear? This girl does!

It was October 3, 2010, my twenty-seventh birthday. *Happy*

birthday to me, I told myself, as I sat in our holding area, waiting to board the plane heading for yet another deployment. It was my third one. How nice of Uncle Sam to give me a round trip ticket to Iraq; just what I wanted, said no one EVER! But there I was, walking in a single-file line towards the plane, clinging to my bookbag to help stop tears from running down my face like a waterfall, wiping them away as fast as they streamed down my cheek. Fear of the unknown filled me. I was heartbroken having to leave my four-year-old daughter with my mother, again, for a year. How did I end up here?

ENLISTING

As a first-generation American whose parents emigrated from Guatemala in their twenties, college was not a topic of discussion in my household. We were your typical Hispanic family. My parents had five children, my father was strict, and my Abue, or grandmother, lived with us. We went to a private Catholic school on the east side of Aurora, Illinois and we owned our own home. Then, when I was around ten years old, my father left us, and our family dynamics instantly changed.

We went from living to surviving. My siblings and I switched from autopilot to survival mode, and we struggled. Overcoming became our norm. Abue ended up taking care of us so that mom could work overtime. Even though my uncle helped us as much as he could, it was tough. At times we had no electricity, had to go to our church pantry for donations, shopped at thrift stores, and used food stamps. We ended up losing our home, but by that time, we were okay with it. We were able to move into a place my mom was able to afford, and it made us stronger. My mother somehow provided the food, shelter, clothing, and everything we needed. I'm grateful for all the sacrifices she had to make along the way.

Fast forward to high school. I'm a product of the West Aurora School District and was your average teenager; a girly-girl, into hair, makeup, and fashion. I didn't take school seriously and instead went to parties. I was the girl who skipped school, hung with friends, and by the time report cards came around, my grades reflected my lack of effort. Senior year came around, and my old friend Fear came around asking me, *What will I do after high school?* None of my friends ever talked about college, and it was not even a word on our radar. I was not prepared at all. I was not filling out admission applications or going on college visits. Instead, my best friend had the great idea of joining the United States Marine Corps her senior year. The enlistment agreement she signed committed her to enter upon graduation.

Senior year, I began attending pool functions with her. A pool function is a training session designed to improve fitness, leadership, and camaraderie before the recruits leave for basic training. I enjoyed the sessions and had decided that I was going to join the Marines too. Graduation was just around the corner, and even though I knew what I wanted to do, Fear crept in. Fear whispered in my ear and told me I wasn't strong enough to be a Marine.

Even though Fear won that round (I didn't wind up joining

the Marines), I knew I still needed a game plan. I started talking to other military branches in hopes that something would be a fit for me. The Navy told me I had to cut my hair, and that was a hard "NO." My father wanted me to join the Air Force, but naturally, I rebelled. So, through my highly sophisticated process of elimination, I decided to join the Army instead. My best friend still enlisted in the Marines and she wound up finishing her service after four years., We are still good friends to this day, even though we served in different military branches.

BASIC TRAINING

June 18, 2002 is the day I left Aurora. Fear was streaming out of my pores. I didn't know what I was getting myself into, but I had nothing to lose. I had to swallow Fear and push forward. Basic training was tough, raw, and required me to give every ounce of my fiber to physical endurance and mental strength. My basic training experience is a story in itself. The words "Yes, Drill Sergeant," "No, Drill Sergeant," "Moving, Drill Sergeant," "Hooah, Drill Sergeant," became the only vocabulary necessary to survive the next nine weeks. Fort Leonard Wood was our base, and sleep was nonexistent because the Army seems to think you only need four hours of sleep. I had to conform to a whole new identity, and it was hard. Janine was gone, and Arriola was born.

The confidence course is a challenging obstacle course, primarily dealing with heights and teamwork. In theory, it's supposed to build self-confidence. However, for me, this was the day everyone in my company got to know who "Arriola" was. As always, Fear tried to resurface again. I'm scared of heights and cried through every single obstacle, and it was the ugly kind of crying. And as if that wasn't enough, it took me forever to run through the course while getting yelled at by the drill sergeants to hurry up. I wanted to quit, as I did throughout my childhood! But it was then and there that I recognized something new. Fear had transformed me from something that used to hold me back into a force that started to push me forward. I thought to myself, *If I don't do this today, I'm going to be back and have to do it all over again tomorrow.* Resilience and determination took over my mind and instead of inhaling Fear, *I exhaled* her.

After my mental victory, I had another defining moment. Once you get past the beginning phase, you move on to "Basic Rifle Marksmanship," which is weaponry training. I wasn't fond of the shooting range because I had to wear my helmet, which consistently slipped down and obstructed my view. My goggles would fog up, sweat dripped down into my eyes, and my elbows and knees would get bruised. These were the intense conditions I had to work under to shoot, "qualify," and pass.

I did the best I could but failed my first qualification. My second go-around was the make-or-break moment. I either passed or got recycled, meaning I would essentially start over. So there I was, under the hot sun, shooting and shooting and shooting, but I could not get it. Then Fear came knocking and reminded me of what was at stake. I took a moment, then walked over to the ammunition shed and sat down. As I sat there, fighting my tears, a butterfly came and landed on my knee. I stared at the butterfly and allowed the Fear to melt away. Magically, faith replaced Fear, and I knew that no matter what happened, everything would be okay. I got up, dusted myself off, and walked back onto the range. I was cocked, locked, and ready to rock.

I walked downrange, grabbed my target, and scored a 24 out of 23. Having overachieved for the first time, I never felt more accomplished than at that very moment. Basic training was emotional and real. It broke me down and then rebuilt me. The girl who went in was not the same girl who came out. Those nine weeks were full of challenges, but that's when I learned that Fear could be positive. She now motivates me.

CONFLICTED MOM

I spent the next few years at Fort Hood, Texas. It took some time for me to adjust to my new reality of active duty. There were rules and regulations for everything; hair couldn't touch the collar, nails could only be a certain length and color, no earrings, boots highly shined, uniform pressed, no hands in your pockets, headgear on if you are outside, and no walking and talking on your cell phone. I joined right after 9/11 so it wasn't long before my first deployment assignment. They needed people to head out to Kuwait; I turned over to my friend and said,

"Let's volunteer and get it out of the way." To my surprise, she agreed. We spent four months in Kuwait and came back relatively unharmed. My first deployment was finished.

Three years after I joined the army, I woke up one morning

sick to my stomach. I thought I was just hungover and stayed in bed to recover. However, my hangover lingered for days, and at that point, I decided to take a pregnancy test. I took the test in the morning, forgot to check the results, and later that night, the word "positive" stopped me in my tracks. My life changed in the blink of an eye. I was twenty-one, unmarried, and not in a real relationship. Fear swallowed me whole as I cried myself to sleep that night.

The next few days was a battle between Fear and my heart; do I keep the baby or not? Do I repeat history and become a single mother, or do I marry the father just because I'm pregnant? Do I stay in the military or get out? I was in Texas with no family; how would I do this? How do I tell my mom that I'm having a baby? My answer to everything was, I don't know. It wasn't until my meeting with the Command Sergeant Major of the base, who was my boss, that I received some clarity. He asked me what was wrong, and I looked at him with tears filling my eyes.

"I'm pregnant," I told him. He walked over and sat down next to me.

"I'm going to talk to you as if you were my daughter," he said. "If this is the only "oops" you've made in your life, you are blessed."

While his message could be misconstrued as him calling my daughter a mistake, I did not receive it in that manner. He was saying that my baby was a blessing, and on March 27, 2006, Amaya, my little girl, was born.

I was now a single mother and still on active duty. I chose

not to marry her father, so the Army moved him to another base (if you are not married, the military has no reason to keep you together). My life felt like a game of chess. I was consistently making moves to figure out motherhood on my own. I was waking up at five o'clock in the morning to get my daughter to daycare and get to the base by six-thirty for morning formation and workout. Then I rushed home to change and was back on base for nine o'clock formation, working all day, completing one more round of evening formation, and then picked up Amaya before six in the evening. On top of that, I sometimes had twenty-four-hour duty, and with no family to help out, I relied on my military friends to help me with overnight and weekend babysitting. I stayed in Fort Hood for most of my career because I feared starting over and rebuilding a network to help me. It was exhausting, but that was my life.

Amaya was around five months old when my next deployment was looming in the distance, to surely threaten my time with her. Fear sprung me into action. I started trying to figure out a way to get a few more months with her. I knew deployment was inevitable, and I wasn't trying to get out of it. It was my duty, and I understood that, but Amaya was an infant; it wasn't right. I jumped through loopholes, talked to anyone who could help me and eventually, I received orders to change units. It bought me a few more months with her, and in 2007, I was ordered to return to Iraq for a fourteen-month deployment. This was my second deployment, my longest time overseas, and the hardest, because it was my first as a mother.

The deployment was heartbreaking. The internet connection in Iraq was weak and Facebook and Skype were fairly new. I heavily depended on phone cards to call back home whenever I could. My daughter and I didn't have the bonding moments most parents get; I didn't have the luxury of seeing her grow and change from month to month. Our phone calls consisted of her little voice saying, "Hi mommy, you in Iraq?" "Yes, mamita, I'm in Iraq."

My service to my country meant I had to sacrifice the most important thing in my life. It meant that I had to watch my daughter grow up without me. That deployment dampened my pride in being a mother because I felt I could never feel like the world's greatest mother. I was gone, and everyone but me was raising her. I had to come to terms with the fact that this was our reality, and it wasn't a stable one.

Even though my time with Amaya was off and on, her strengths carried me through. The military gave me job security which allowed me to provide for her, unfortunately, from a distance. And while I could have gotten out of the military, it was Fear that kept me in—Fear of the civilian world, and Fear of not being able to make it in the outside world. So, I kept reenlisting. Fear kept me in the military longer than I would have liked to stay.

STARTING OVER

That's how I got here, about to take off for deployment number three. I took my seat on the plane and settled in for a long flight. We landed in Kuwait, and a few days later, we flew out to Iraq, where I spent the next eleven months. The military life came with sacrifices, including my identity as a mother. I missed major milestone moments with Amaya. However, military life also gave me pride in serving my country and taught me resilience, leadership, strength, deep-rooted friendships, and skills I doubt I would have acquired anywhere else. To this day, I don't regret my military experience. However, I do regret staying in it longer than I should have. It wasn't until Amaya was almost six when I was able to finally be present in her life. She became a mesmerizing young lady—independent, smart, loving, and funny.

Shortly after that deployment, I left the military and found myself making the difficult decision to start over. I had to change career paths, find out who I was without the military, and go back to school. I battled with Fear every step of the way, second-guessing myself, making excuses, having imposter syndrome, and questioning my decisions. Yet, by this time, I knew how to harness Fear and turn her into my motivator. Now, I love how she pushes me to become my best self and overall, I am thankful for her. Without Fear, I wouldn't have the memories and experiences that have shaped me throughout the years. I have learned it's not always about being fearless sometimes; it's about *fearing*-less.

THINK YOUNG AND GROW

A few years ago, I came across the phrase, "Year of Yes." It was a podcast on Super Soul Sunday when Oprah interviewed author Shonda Rhimes who wrote the book, *Year of Yes: How to*

Dance It Out, Stand in the Sun, and Be Your Own Person." On the podcast, she talked about how she used to say no to opportunities that were outside of her comfort zone. I resonated with that because in the past, I would say no because of Fear. I decided to take Shonda's advice and say yes to opportunities that scared me. My senior year in college was my personal "year of yes." I took advantage of every opportunity available, and by the end of the year, I had presented my first undergraduate research project, built strong relationships, applied and was accepted into graduate school, and got my first job in higher education.

I am still in the practice of saying yes, and the opportunities keep rolling in. I climbed my first mountain which was twelve thousand feet high, even though I'm scared of heights, I'm writing this short story, I presented at my first higher education conference, and I graduated with my master's degree. I challenge you to do a year of yes when opportunities come that bring you fear, take a leap of faith, and say yes.

THIS IS ME

I am Janine Arriola a Guatemalan-American and a U.S. Army veteran with three deployments under my belt. I am an alumna of North Central College, where I earned both my Master of Leadership in Higher Education and a bachelor's degree in sports management. I am currently working in higher education, helping other veterans start on their college journey. I love outdoor recreational hobbies, traveling, laughing until you cry, breaking generational barriers, and have a passion for diversity, inclusion, and equality. I want my story to remind young Latinas that they are not their circumstances; son fuerte y poderosas! I hopes to inspire minds to set their soul on fire with their passions, regardless of the obstacles that may appear.

In my wildest dreams, I would work for the government.

THE FIVE-YEAR PLAN

1. Work on my J.Lo. and Shakira mom body
2. Earn a doctorate degree
3. Not settle for less!

LA PLATICADORA

Lissete Aguirre Ochoa

"Let the people that you invite into your life enrich and invigorate it."

"Lissete loves to talk with everyone around her," said my elementary school teacher to my mom and I during parent/teacher conferences. Of course, my mom agreed with her and scolded me when we left the meeting. *"No seas tan platicadora en la escuela y pon atención."* (Don't be so talkative at school and pay attention!) Little did I know that my mom's scolding could not stop the future career of this little social butterfly from unfolding.

FIND YOUR TRIBE

My parents immigrated to the United States from Mexico. My father came when he was seventeen and my mother arrived when she was eighteen years old. Like many of our parents, they came to the U.S. with so many hopes and dreams, but one of them was always to provide a better future for their kids. My parents always stressed the importance of family and good friends. Seeing them value their relationships with others influenced me to build strong bonds with those in my life.

I'm from a typical, large Mexican family, so I'm lucky enough to have siblings, *primas,* and *primos* (cousins) who are great friends and my support and backbone. As a young girl, I sometimes would struggle with school anxiety and building friendships with my peers, but my parents would always remind me that I had a whole tribe of family members that were also my friends.

As a first-generation college student, I knew that the pressure of graduating with a degree was not just for my parents and family, but to also serve as a role model for my younger family members as well. I'm proud to say that I feel like I did accomplish this because many of my younger cousins went on to enroll and graduate from college.

When I was younger, I would always say I wanted to be a teacher, which is why I initially studied elementary education as a freshman at Northern Illinois University (NIU). Very early on, I knew that I wanted to work with and help students. Throughout my college education, I realized there were other positions within education that I was more passionate about, like being a high school counselor. The eagerness to talk and communicate with others never went away, and I knew that this would be the perfect career choice for me. I could continue on being the platicadora that I've always been.

When I started college, I went in with a completely different mindset than I had in high school. Back then, I hadn't gotten as involved as I would've liked. I always avoided joining school clubs or sports, because I wasn't "popular enough" or athletically skilled enough. As soon as I turned 16, I started working a part-time job at a local fast food restaurant. I devoted my extra free time to work and slowly build an income for myself. This allowed me to gain responsibility and independence, but it also taught me how to multitask effectively.

When I started at NIU, I knew that I needed to get involved with campus activities not only to grow and network, but also to establish positive relationships in my life. I've found that friendships can take a lot of work and communication, but if you can find a solid group that can grow with you through life's battles, those are the friends that are worth cherishing and keeping forever.

Before going to college, I had never heard of a sorority. When I did, I thought it was this weird cult that you saw on TV. TV shows always seemed to portray sororities as just a social club and I never really knew the purpose. Luckily for me, that wasn't the case. I joined a diverse and multicultural group of confident women that I knew would help me dive into the leadership opportunities that I craved. Joining Sigma Lambda Gamma was undoubtedly the best college decision that I could have made. Not only did I gain strong leadership skills and incredible networking opportunities with NIU administration that led to immense scholarships, but I met some of my best friends that will forever be family.

Through hard work, I graduated from NIU with both

a Bachelor of Arts degree in sociology and a master's degree of science in education in counseling. There is no way I could have accomplished this without my family and college friends, who became my second family. Sometimes friends, and people in general, are meant to be in your life for a specific reason and season. These can be childhood friendships or romantic relationships. I've had friends that I initially thought would be lifelong friendships, but as we grew, we also changed, and those friendships fizzled with change. We are constantly evolving and sometimes we just simply outgrow people. Don't let these losses get in the way of your continual growth; continue to look positively into the future.

Let the people that you invite into your life enrich and invigorate it. There's truly something to be said about having solid friendships within a dynamic group of people to help you gain wisdom and continue to develop into who you are meant to be. My tribe has always been there to support and encourage me during tough times, but they've also been there to celebrate my triumphs too. They've been there for academic accomplishments, family celebrations, and given me valuable relationship advice and personal advice with my life's decision making. It's so important to surround yourself with positive energy and those who motivate you to follow your goals and dreams.

TRUST YOUR PROCESS

One counseling technique that I learned early on in my training is to have the student/patient discuss their story without any interruption from the facilitator. This is very hard to do, especially when you want to talk and share your opinion as much as I do. However, you as the facilitator, have to trust the counseling process and let the student/patient guide their own healing. I constantly think about that and remind myself as well. Many times, it's so easy to give advice to others; it's not as easy to follow the same advice in your own life.

Throughout my early twenties, I was never worried about the stress of societal norms on women. To say that I traveled through life to the beat of my own drum is an understatement. My goal was, and always has been, to make my parents proud and have a fulfilling career that makes me happy.

However, as I approached the age of thirty, I started giving into the pressure that our culture and society places on women. I saw friends and family establishing their careers, getting married, and starting their families. Luckily, I have a partner who didn't act on that pressure, was understanding, and had beliefs similar to mine. My mother always shared the wisdom of her own life's experiences and encouraged me to trust my own process and path. I made my life decisions on my own time and terms, and my tribe backed me up.

Once I got married, the societal pressure really kicked in; everyone was waiting for us to buy a house, have a successful marriage and career, and start a family. The pressure was greatest from certain family members because in our Mexican culture, the traditional gender roles are still strong. It seems like as soon as you get married, the very next day they want you to have a baby.

However, like anything else in life, there's no guide on how to make all this possible.

All around me others made it look so easy, but in my mind, I knew that we had to take it slowly and trust our own process. In opening up about my struggles with others, I realized that building the perfect life was not as easy as others make it look. I had been comparing my life and my struggles to an ideal, and slowly, the stress was getting to me. So much so that unfortunately, I suffered a miscarriage.

At first, we tried to put the miscarriage to the side and continue with life, almost as if it didn't happen. However, as time went on it became harder and harder to deny that it had a true impact on our lives. For a while, I hid this secret inside, and it nearly killed me. It wasn't until I truly opened up about the loss that I began to heal. Through my communication and conversations with friends, colleagues, and family members, I gained stronger bonds with those who unfortunately, shared the same experience as me. Their words of encouragement and support were so therapeutic. My tribe was growing.

My husband and I have always wanted a family, and although the pregnancy was unexpected, we will continue trying to make this dream of ours a reality. In healing, I realized that I had never wanted a baby more after going through my miscarriage. In the social media era that we live in, we see many "perfect" lives but oftentimes, we don't talk about the taboo, unpleasant realities that sometimes go with them. Miscarriage is one of those.

I've learned that life will not always go as planned and obstacles that may appear as huge mountains and seem impossible to overcome are simply bumps in the road that will make us stronger. I've also learned that the saying is true; we can't judge a book by its cover. We now live in a world where we have different platforms available to us and we must use those for good to truly be the change that we wish to make in the world.

MANIFEST YOUR GOALS AND DREAMS

Life is too short to be anything but happy. As much as we would like to have everything planned and figured out, things don't always happen as expected. It's important to reflect and be grateful but also to manifest your goals and dreams. Speak them into the universe! Don't let the comparison game or fear stop you from reaching your goals. God placed certain things in your life for you to pursue them. Live your best life and watch God open doors for you.

Sometimes we can be our own worst critics, and we all have a story that will be filled with ups and downs, but it's important to believe in positivity. Great things happen when you least expect them. It's important to work hard, dream big, and have a positive outlook.

THINK YOUNG AND GROW

I'm all about post-it notes and lists. I have them everywhere and I use them to help me manifest my aspirations. They are constant reminders to myself that positive things can happen and are coming, but they're also simple forms of gentle, self-encouragement.

I challenge you to make something visual for your life that is a reminder of the dreams you want to manifest. It can be a drawing, a vision board, or even just some post-its with ideas and to-do items that will lead to your dream. Put it somewhere you will see it every day and let it inspire you all week.

THIS IS ME

I am a 32-year-old Mexican-American born in Chicago, but raised in Franklin Park. I am the youngest of three siblings and have been married since 2017. My husband and I live on a small farm in the suburbs and spend a lot of time outdoors with our dogs, chickens, and horses. In my free time, I love hanging out with family and friends and chatting our lives away!

I have a bachelor of arts degree in sociology and a master's of science degree in counseling. I started my counseling career working at a non-profit community counseling agency in 2011 and it was such an eye-opening experience. I have been a high school counselor since 2012 and my mission has always been to work with underrepresented students to help them achieve their post-secondary plans. I am passionate about working with high school students and hope to continue this work as long as I can. I'm constantly looking for ways to grow professionally and will start taking some additional classes soon to broaden my knowledge on the counseling field. The *platicadora* in me has never fizzled and is just getting started on her dreams!

I hope to start a family while continuing to influence the younger generation that I currently work with.

THE FIVE-YEAR PLAN

1. Travel and explore different cultures
2. Continue with my education
3. Build a business with my husband

DIAMONDS ARE MADE UNDER PRESSURE

Kateryn Ferreira

"Remember, everything looks impossible until it is done."

Adversity brings out the courage and bravery in us. At times, we have no choice but to fight back and win. The lessons and strength you gain throughout the process is what makes you better equipped for the next battle.

COVID-19 has drastically changed our lives. Lives have been lost, milestones and events have been cancelled/postponed, people have been laid off their jobs, education is no longer what it used to be, supermarkets shelves are half empty and most of us are stuck at home. Our daily living has become so foreign and restricted that we feel like we are living in a movie. This pandemic has been a mental, emotional, and social burden to us all.

ESSENTIAL AND STRUGGLING

As an essential worker at the local hospital, I had to wake up bright and early every day to be at work. Thankfully, as an administrative staff, I was not directly working with COVID-19 patients. At first it was very hurtful and terrifying to walk into the hospital. However, throughout April and May, I noticed my devotion and purpose as an essential worker. However, as I walked into the hospital every day, I risked my life and the life of my loved ones at home. This really had taken a toll on my mental and emotional health. As I roamed the hallways of the hospital, I felt the burden of loss of lives each day. My coworkers shared experiences and encounters with body bags being transported through the hospital. This grief and fear were felt by everyone. Unfortunately, thousands of New Yorkers died, including many African American, Hispanics and Latinos, elderly people and people who have other chronic health conditions. These groups are at greater risk of complication and death.

In the middle of this pandemic, I asked myself, when did this happen? How did we get here? How did our daily lives change so drastically, that we are now obsessively on alert and continually wearing a mask, gloves, and staying six feet away from everyone around us? I couldn't even hug the friends who are dear to me at work. We felt helpless. The one mission that we had, to improve the health and quality of life of our patients, was no longer feasible because we had an enemy that was working ten times faster than us, taking the lives of so many around us.

Honestly, I am unsure how I managed to juggle, work, family, school, and COVID-19. I know I made it through because diamonds are made under pressure. Every morning I woke up with a goal, and every night was an accomplishment. I kept myself busy and positive, this technique really helped me get through these devastating times. I listened to Joel Osteen, an American pastor who has really helped me be hopeful and faithful about the future. In addition to enhancing my faith and mental health, I also used my social platforms to meet people and network. Networking and socializing with people who are successful in their field really inspired me to move forward and be positive about what the future held.

Despite all the strategies and techniques, I was forced to build through this pandemic, I had to cope with additional losses. Unfortunately, I lost two special relatives during this pandemic who were very dear to my heart. Salome Rosado, also known as Mama Salo, was an aunt, a mother, my babysitter since birth, a friend, and an amazing human being that was always willing to lend a hand to those who needed her help. Furthermore, she was elderly with health issues, but if it wasn't for COVID-19, I believe she would still be here with us today.

According to family, she contracted the virus during her visits to the doctors. Initially, she had trouble breathing. They took her in for an x-ray and she was diagnosed with pneumonia. Shortly afterward, she tested positive for COVID-19. After five worrisome days of being admitted and connected to a ventilator, her heart stopped. They called her daughter, Carmen Rosado, the morning of April 1, 2020, to share the devastating news.

That day was one of the saddest days of my life. I couldn't believe it because just days before, we had been told she was getting better. However, her body apparently wasn't able to resist the virus and it severely affected her heart. May she rest in peace.

Mama Salo, you will always remain in our hearts. I love you.

A month later, I found out my dad was having an affair with a young woman in the Dominican Republic, and she was pregnant. This news tore me into pieces. My dad has always been my hero, my role model, and the person I respect and admire. Growing up, you have this image of your dad, as a faithful and loyal male, but he broke my heart. As a daddy's girl, I confronted him about it. He didn't confirm that the baby was his. However, this has been devastating and disappointing. I felt betrayed but how do I stop reaching out and showing him how much I love him? He is my dad. I know, I have to accept this and accept this decision. This situation and my feelings about it might come out as naive to some people. However, this really has marked me as his daughter and as a woman.

Just days after I found out about my dad's situation, my grandmother, my dad's mother died. On June 6, 2020, Mama Ada, also known as Yolanda Adaglisa Vargas De Ferreira, passed away in the Dominican Republic, leaving the hearts of her children and grandchildren empty and full of sorrow. My grandmother had multiple strokes in just a few days. She was also hypertensive and diabetic. There were many comorbidities, however, we were not expecting to lose her like that. She was so sweet and attentive and would always greet us with warm hugs, her warm presence, and delicious meals. Many of her children and grandchildren live here in the United States, Pennsylvania, and New York. Due to COVID-19 regulations and restrictions, we weren't able to travel to Dominican Republic to gather with family, grieve, and attend her burial. This grief and sorrow were more than I could describe in writing. It has been six days since her death and I still can't process that she is gone. Mama, I miss you so much! I love you!

All of the loss, the emotional and mental burden of everyday life has been unbearable. However, despite it all, I have continued to find the strength within me to surpass all this pain. I know I will be stronger and greater in the future. I know this because I have overcome many obstacles in the past. Losing loved ones has been life changing and has marked my life forever, but I also know both my aunt and grandmother are in a better place today. They will always be in my heart as the angelic individuals they were and will continue to be. With all the love, they left and shared with us here on earth, I will persist, I will conquer, I will empower, I will overcome, I will thrive, I will inspire. I believe I can, and I will continue pushing for my family, my friends, and my angels above, Mama Ada and Mama Salo. I will continue pushing for a greater tomorrow, for me and my future, because I know I can, and I am halfway there. Being hopeful and positive about my future has always been my fuel to keep pushing.

BEING BEST DURING THE WORST

During the global health crisis, I worked hard to rise above. I took the adversity and turned it into a good phase in my life. I worked out with my little sister and spent more time with her. I did this out of diversion and as a survival technique. However, I wanted to keep my sister motivated and active. She spent all her time at home, and this could have been a very detrimental time for her. In addition to exercise, I ate healthier and fed my mind and soul with positive vibes and information. I successfully completed my MPH (Master in Public Health degree), scrambling through assignments, working full-time, meal prepping, working out, being a good partner, dog mom, and sister.

In addition to coping, dealing with COVID-19, family loss and conflicts, America is dealing with racism and protests against police brutality. It would be wrong to not mention the loss and grief, we share as African Americans and Latinos. Racism is something that is still ever-present in our lives. It affects us, our friends, family, and future children. This too is a public health crisis that should be addressed as an urgent and threatening issue. Racism against African American and people of color needs to stop. This should not be the future of our country. During protests, we have witnessed devastating destruction of businesses, looting, arson, and fighting. In my opinion, this is not the correct way to fight for our rights and police brutality. It fails to give a perception of dignity and identify for what we stand for. We have to do better. Everyone in America—White, Asian, Native American, African American—all need to do better. I am hopeful for the future of America's unity and the end of this pandemic.

During all these events, I felt overwhelmed by my feelings of loss and my surroundings. Thankfully, I was able to step out of my head and notice that I couldn't let this affect my progress and success. I had to stay grounded and make sure I was doing things that made me happy and identify my values, beliefs, and who I am as a person. Every task looks surreal until you dive into it and make it a reality. With the deaths of my relatives, the new social norms of COVID-19, family conflict, and social destruction, it is very difficult to get up and continue to believe. Trust me when I say it is difficult. Sometimes I have to take my own advice and apply it. Life is hard and unpredictable, but if we keep moving forward and motivating ourselves and others to be better, we will have a sense of accomplishment and happiness.

I know I can bear this time in my life. Every time you feel the same as I do, you have to stand up and believe you can surpass any obstacle. We sometimes take our lives for granted. We should never do so because there are others who are going through something far worse than we are or have even less than what we have. You should always keep four candles lit in your heart: appreciation, hope, faith, and courage. With these four candles, you will excel to greater things. There is something greater than me, that watches me and gives me the strength and direction I need. Since I was very young, I have always been goal driven. I love progress, growth, overcoming, and becoming. I love to check boxes and follow to do lists which I highlight and cross out. Achieving goals is so satisfying to me, no matter how small the task. These small actions are what keep me sane and moving forward.

On a brighter note, I took this time to self-reflect. I pondered the question, what is it that I have been wanting to do for a very long time and haven't taken the time to do? Despite all the hardships in front of me, I had amazing revelations and pushed myself to do positive acts. I have connected with amazing entrepreneurs who have become mentors and friends. They have encouraged me to fulfill my dreams and have given me the opportunity to do so. I started writing articles with former professors and this publication.

Thanks to Jacqueline Camacho Ruiz, CEO of Fig Factor Media. During hard times, life also presents you with opportunities, guiding angels, and pathways of growth. Jackie was one of my guardian angels. Thank you, Jackie. Jackie is an amazing, hardworking Latina that has devoted her life to inspiring and elevating others with her magic. I definitely want to follow in Jackie's footsteps in the near future, to use my drive to inspire others to grow and encourage them not to let their fears, obstacles, and circumstances keep them away from meeting their full potential in life.

During this time, I have also joined the Niños de la Caridad Foundation as a board member. We help immigrant families in the Bronx, access educational and social resources in the community and guide youth to excel in high school to successfully gain entry into college to meet their career goals. Being part of this foundation really fills me with love and passion. I have been given the opportunity to give back to my community while tailoring resources, educating, and empowering our communities to advocate for themselves and excel.

I have learned that even when you feel like there is no hope and everything around you doesn't make sense or is not going as expected, you must continue to be brave and have the courage to break out of that mentality and make a change in your life. Start a business, develop relationships, travel the world, write that book, buy that house, and believe in yourself. You must push yourself to be great because no one else can do it for you.

Remember, everything looks impossible until it is done. What keeps me going is understanding that my feelings and my current experiences are all temporary. Most of my emotions of anger, frustration, and negativity will most likely be irrelevant a year from now. So why spend time dwelling on something that will not benefit you in the future? Surpass that feeling and develop emotional competence. It is important to be aware of your feelings. That is what has helped me. You should try it!

MOTIVATE AND SUCCEED

Motivation and courage are key during progress. However, going through all the obstacles I have faced in the last few months, I had a lack of motivation some days. Those are the days I felt the need to push harder. Consistency then overrules motivation. Therefore, focus on being consistent. Push yourself that extra mile so when you lose motivation, it has already become second nature to proceed. Don't let that day stop you from exceeding the next day's to-do list. Adversity has been fundamental to my growth, persistence, and future success. Adversity, courage and the ability to overcome, keeps you going. When times get tough, keep pushing.

Surround yourself with positive content. Watch TED Talks, videos, movies, read an inspirational book, network through LinkedIn and other social platforms, listen to a podcast, follow a religious figure. There are endless channels of positivity out there…… so use them to your advantage. Remember, the best version of you is on the other side of your comfort zone.

THINK YOUNG AND GROW

Please take a moment and write down all of your short-term and long-term goals, for today, this week, this month, this year, and the next five to ten years. Visualize them, embrace the work it will take for you to achieve these goals, and how happy you will be once you achieve them. Most importantly, embrace the courage, bravery, and discipline it will take to get you where you want to be.

Life is not a destination; it is a journey, so if you wake up every day with a positive and progressive mindset, you will fulfill all you were created to be. If you find yourself feeling a bit overwhelmed by all your goals and a long to-do list, my advice to you is to take the first step and act. It doesn't matter how small or insignificant you think the step might be. Make that phone call, start writing that book, do the research, start your own brand! Step out of your comfort zone and the rest will be history! As Newt Gingrich said, "Perseverance is the hard work you do after you get tired of doing the hard work you already did."

Finally, I want to also challenge you to reach out to five experts this week. These individuals could be professionals in your field of interest or not. You will be surprised by who knows who and how they could connect you to the right person who can transform your future. In addition, it will also build up your network and your confidence.

THIS IS ME

My name is Kateryn Ferreira. I am Dominican, born and raised in Washington Heights. I completed my Bachelor of Science degree in health service administration with Magna Cum Laude honors at CUNY School of Lehman College. I just completed my Master in Public Health (MPH) in community health education at CUNY School of Public Health and Health Policy.

I worked as a full-time program assistant at Montefiore Medical Center in the Bronx. I have more than six years of experience in the health field, including experience in customer service, community outreach, and program management. I also have my own businesses in direct marketing as an independent consultant for Touchstone Crystal by Swarovski, Farmasi, and Pure Romance. I am a board member of Niños De La Caridad Foundation in the Bronx, helping and empowering our immigrant and Hispanic families to access resources and services that facilitate future education for their children.

My dream is to found an organization that promotes both sexual and mental wellness in youth, adolescence years are known to be crucial in both development and future life decisions. This organization will help us empower and inspire youth to achieve their dreams through mentorship, networking, and self-development while addressing both sexual and mental wellness.

THE FIVE-YEAR PLAN

1. Become the founder of my own youth development organization
2. Travel the world
3. Empower and inspire youth to achieve their dreams through mentorship, networking, and self-development

MARIPOSA

Claudia Georgina Martinez

"There is always a lesson or something to gain from hardship"

When I think about growing up, I remember the immense loneliness I felt, the feeling of not belonging, being misunderstood, and that nobody was there for me. As I experienced life, this feeling remained with me more than I ever expected.

My family called me *enojona*. I was always yelling to be heard because I never felt like I was. But all along I was just a child that needed nurturing, a hug, a kiss, more love, or someone to tell me that everything was going to be okay.

Today I can say that all of this has built me into the woman I am. I've bloomed. I am resilient. I am strong. I am a warrior. I am like a *mariposa*, (butterfly) who spent time in a cocoon, only to emerge stronger than ever and able to soar to great heights.

CATERPILLAR

I was born in, Acámbaro, Guanajuato, Mexico, prematurely, with a heart condition. The doctors said either my heart could close and heal, or I would have lifelong problems. Thankfully, it healed. I was the middle of three sisters and considered myself a somewhat happy child, despite the childhood trauma I experienced. I've always been a good student, getting stars since kindergarten and excelling in school. However, I was missing something: my dad. Like a lot of Latino families, my dad went to work in the U.S to be able to provide for us back in Mexico.

By the time I was born, my dad had been coming and going to the U.S for about seven years in search of a better life. Because of this, during the first year of my life, I grew up only seeing my dad once a year at Christmas. I truly admire my dad because he went from selling chicles (chewing gum) and newspapers in the streets of Mexico to working as a self-employed mechanic.

The hardest thing about not having him there every day was feeling like I had no one to love or comfort me. My mother suffered from depression which made her both emotionally and physically absent. She would leave my younger sister and me with my older sister, who was only eight alone at home, to go sell Avon or gold. This made me feel alone and insecure, with no mother or father to tell me that everything was going to be okay. As an adult, I have been able to work on healing this part of me. I have discovered that love is something I can give myself first, and then give it to others and get in return.

I remember the day that my mom told me we were leaving

Acámbaro and going to the U.S. My dad had applied for our green cards when I was only one year old, and we were finally approved seven years later. I cried non-stop and said I didn't want to go. I didn't want to leave my friends, my family, or my town. It was all I knew.

I remember my first day in Chicago like it was yesterday. As I walked into the beautiful house my dad had purchased for us, I said aloud, "We're rich now!" In Mexico, we lived in a humble, adobe home. So to me this was huge. But everything else about moving to the U.S., like starting over as an eight-year-old who did not know the language and customs of the new country, was extremely difficult.

I was demoted a grade just because I didn't know the language. But thankfully, I later went to a school with a great bilingual program and was moved a grade up. In school, I was bullied because of my weight and because I could not speak English. I remember crying a lot and wanting to go back to Mexico. Both of my parents had to work to sustain the household, so this meant they were not around for most of the day. I remember coming home from school and cooking for myself. I eventually improved my English by watching educational cartoons like the Berenstain Bears.

Things were bad at school but worse at home. My parents would constantly fight, and I would lock myself in my room and wish I were somewhere else. To make matters worse, my mom would sometimes call me fat without knowing how much it affected me. This loneliness and lack of love contributed to developing anorexia at the age of twelve. I was placed in both inpatient and outpatient treatments.

In treatment, I finally felt like I was being seen and that my family cared. However, my disorder morphed into bulimia. I felt very alone dealing with these disorders but eventually, I recovered and was able to carry on like the warrior I was born to be.

In middle school, I started getting more involved. I joined everything I could and was involved in Student Council, Beta Club, French Club, Orchestra, Sports, and Poms Squad. Slowly I started missing Mexico less, assimilating into the culture, and focusing more on school. To me, it was clear that my dad had brought us to this country for a chance at a better life. To achieve it, though, he worked three jobs, my mom worked two, and we hardly saw either of them.

Because of this, I pushed myself and did extremely well in high school because I wanted a different life. I graduated in the top ten percent of my class and received an automatic, two-year full-tuition scholarship to the community college near my home, but also applied for a state scholarship that was only given to three students every year. To my surprise, I GOT IT! I remember how proud I was when I heard the news. Because of this, I decided to attend the University of Illinois at Chicago and become the first person in my family to go to college. I didn't know what the future entailed, how to navigate college life, or how to get along in the city. Even so, I knew it was time to leave my sheltered life.

METAMORPHOSIS

Before deciding on UIC, I had considered attending fashion school to become a designer but decided not to; I wanted a career that was more secure. At UIC, I feared I would get lost. Then I found the LARES (Latin American Recruitment and Educational Services) program which helped me transition to college with a summer program where I met some of my best friends. It was a huge comfort to meet other first-generation students who shared so many of my feelings and experiences. I knew absolutely NOTHING except that I had to graduate, but I soon discovered that my scholarship only covered tuition and not room and board, so I had to take out loans for the rest of my expenses.

I needed to stay clear of my toxic family environment to make something of myself. Doing so didn't mean I didn't love my family. I hoped to build stronger, healthier relationships with them while living on campus.

In college, I experienced everything for the first time—parties, drinking, city life, and what I thought was love. I fell for someone so hard, the relationship held me back from experiencing college to its fullest, which ultimately fueled my low self-esteem. I was broken inside, with only my friends to hold me up.

Eventually, I decided to study something that combined my creativity and interest in business: marketing. Some of the courses were a struggle. I even failed my accounting class which made me doubt myself and my capabilities. I felt like there was something wrong with me. But today I can tell you, don't let a class define you or your future.

I still managed to excel. I joined Her Campus, an online magazine for college women, and became the editor-in-chief. I joined LABS (the Latinos Association for Business Students) and became the marketing director. I was involved with Boohoo.com on campus, where we threw amazing fashion shows, and I was also was part of the founding board for a scholarship for Latinos on campus.

Looking back, I was juggling a lot in college. I worked three jobs at one point to make money since my parents could not really give me much. After my first year on campus, I feared I would have to move home and commute. Luckily, I found an off-campus housing option called La Casa Student Housing. I was able to move in, take on a part-time internship, receive free housing, and most importantly, not have to move home.

I made it my goal to get an internship every semester. I interned for Akira in Chicago, The Resurrection Project, Telemundo, and even earned an all-expenses paid internship in New York City for the summer after my junior year. Afterwards, I only had one more semester before graduating. I wasn't really prepared for what came next. I had friends who had already secured jobs to start after graduation, and I hadn't even started my job hunt yet.

On the day of my graduation, I remember feeling joy, happiness, and pride. Like a movie playing in my head, I remembered all of the tests, sleepless night, and internships.

When they called my name to walk across the stage, I smiled and turned to see my family. All of my hard work had paid off. This accomplishment was not only for me, but for them. I was the first of us to earn a college degree.

SPREADING MY WINGS AND FLYING

Unfortunately, I was unable to find a job for some time, so I moved back home. For six unsuccessful months, I felt like there was something wrong with me. College may give you a degree, but it doesn't equip you with the tools you need to succeed in life.

One day, I decided to reach out to Jackie Camacho. I had met her during a keynote presentation she gave while I was in college. She told me to come to her home so that we could talk. I walked into her house, nervous, but driven to change my circumstance. Deep down inside, I knew there was more to life than my current situation. The first thing she asked me was, "How can I help you?" I will NEVER forget it because it was the first time anyone had really extended their hand to help me like that. After a conversation about my struggle, she suggested I apply to the Fig Factor Foundation, her nonprofit mentoring organization. She said it could help me immensely. To this day, Jackie says she remembers the sparkle in my eyes and says she could see my hunger to change the world. It was a moment that changed the trajectory of my life.

At the Fig Factor Foundation, I met great people and was hired by Jackie as an intern to work at her firm, JJR Marketing. After a few months, I knew I wanted to stay long-term, but just couldn't get myself to ask. I called my Fig Factor Foundation mentor who encouraged me and said," All you need is thirty seconds of insane courage." I took a deep breath and told myself I could do it. I called Jackie, asked for a full-time job and my new journey as a marketing coordinator at JJR began. I moved out of the house and found an apartment in the city. There, I worked my way up to project manager, and was learning a lot. It was there that I built the foundation to my career before taking another leap of faith and believing in myself to look for more.

Again, I struggled to get hired, even though I went on multiple interviews. This affected my confidence and I spiraled into a depression. I couldn't see the light at the end of the tunnel and would end up crying or tired most of the time. *Why is this happening to me a second time?* I would ask myself. *Why me? Am I not good enough to get another job? What is wrong with me"* These thoughts clogged my mind. I would see close friends securing amazing jobs and I would get jealous because I felt that I deserved that too. But this only isolated me from them.

Out of desperation, I started doing something I never thought I would do. I started driving for Lyft. I felt ashamed because I wasn't using my degree, but then I thought of everything my parents had done to succeed. I thought of all the hunger, the obstacles, and remembered something I heard someone say once: *"Con la pena, no se come."* (With embarrassment, you don't eat.)

Over the next few years, I landed a position as a project manager, but soon discovered that the environment was quite toxic. I stayed as long as I could, for the money, but finally had to put my mental health first and quit. Simultaneously, I was dealing with some deteriorating relationships, partly due to my inability to deal with them in the midst of all my other problems.

Again, I found myself doing Lyft but this time, it felt better. I knew I needed support to make it on my own so I decided to call a woman-centered resource center and found a therapist. My healing journey began. While in therapy, I enrolled in a leadership program with Global Leadership and really worked on healing and growing. I met amazing people and started dating my boyfriend, Roberto, and working with his mom, Gemma, at her flower shop. I helped manage her shop and was even able to offer my marketing skills. It wasn't a highly paid job, but I received invaluable experience and I made a difference for a small, start-up business. She also gave me the motherly love I had so lacked and craved as I was growing up. It still makes me very emotional to this day, but I now understand that some people come into our lives to teach us or to help us heal. Gemma showed me the genuine love of a mother.

CALIFORNIA CALLING

Soon after, Roberto and I decided to move to California. I had just turned 26 and had already moved three times on my own. Moving to California was an easy, yet hard decision for me. I knew it was the right thing to do and Roberto's love was unconditional. However, I was my family's rock. They always turned to me for help and support. In so many ways, I felt responsible for them. But I was ready for a fresh start and wanted to leave all the hurt in Chicago. I had to let go.

I was only able to say goodbye to my dad. He gave me his blessing once again, just like the first time I had moved away from home with a bag full of dreams. I knew it was time to open my wings fully and fly, even as we got into the car and set out for our cross-country road trip to our new home.

I arrived with little to no savings, no permanent apartment, and no job. I decided to start doing what I knew was easy, fast money: driving for Lyft. I could start almost immediately while I sought another job. While job hunting, I would tell myself repeatedly that I was strong, capable, and confident. I knew I was destined for greatness. A month later, I had secured a job within my dream company, Univision. Confidence really does go a long way, but only when we first believe in and love ourselves.

My journey in California continues and I encourage you too to take a risk and have faith because you never know where it will lead you. All you need is thirty seconds of insane courage. Let's break the stigmas around mental health and therapy. Let's break the chains of intergenerational trauma. That's what I want to do so that my future children will live a happier life.

There are no coincidences. Everything is happening as it should. Even when you don't understand why things are happening. Trust life and trust the process. But especially, always trust yourself. Be your biggest advocate, cheerleader, and love yourself. Believe in yourself. When I was going through all the pain, I didn't understand why, but now I know that there was a bigger purpose. Now I say, "This is happening FOR ME not TO ME." I invite you to do the same.

I am stronger today because of that dark time in my life. This journey has shown me that I am like a lotus flower who blooms most beautifully from the thickest of mud. I am a better friend, daughter, and girlfriend because of everything I went through. Today I am more grateful because I have realized there is always a lesson or something to gain from hardship. I have embraced my hardships as a part of me, but they do not define me. Above all, I want you to know that if you're reading this and feel alone, please know that you are not. Keep fighting and believing. I love you. I believe in you. You are destined for greatness.

CHALLENGE

I would like to leave you with three things. I hope you try one or all.

1. No matter where you are in life, you can make an impact in someone else's world. Someone once told me, "I believe in you," and now I make sure to say this to others who may need to hear it. Help someone move forward, make that connection, push their resume to the top if you can, or simply tell them, "I believe in you." It may be the first time they ever hear it. Let's show more empathy towards others.
2. Practice self-care, which is also self-love. This has helped me immensely. Make a drawing or list of things you can do whenever you need some self-care and are feeling stressed or anxious. For example, dancing to music you love, reading positive affirmations (make sure you include these!), or stretching.

3. Create a Gratitude Jar. Gratitude is the best way to get back into a positive mindset or stay in one. Fill a Mason Jar with things you are grateful for and take one out every time you are feeling down.

THIS IS ME

I am Claudia Georgina Martinez Perez, a resilient, hard-working, young Latina determined to leave a legacy in this world and lead with a heart full of love, empathy, and happiness.

I am an immigrant from Acámbaro, Guanajuato. I am a first-generation college graduate from the University of Illinois at Chicago where I graduated with a degree in marketing and a minor in promotions and communications. Through my life experiences I have become passionate about destigmatizing mental health issues, especially in the Latino community.

I believe we are not defined by our past trauma. We are not defined by the circumstances that surround us. I am determined to break the generational trauma that my family has carried for generations. I want everyone to know that love really does heal everything. I am passionate about helping others achieve their goals and success. I am passionate about storytelling, travel, and music/dance.

Currently, I am working at Univision Creator Network, the number one leading Latino-focused creator network in the U.S. I live in California with my loving and supportive boyfriend, Roberto.

> *To become a successful, impactful entrepreneur, international speaker, author, podcaster, and philanthropist who inspires others to heal their intergenerational trauma and live a fulfilled life so they can be love and light to the world.*

THE FIVE-YEAR PLAN

1. Travel the world (maybe with my parents and grandparents) and reach financial independence
2. Run a successful and profitable business (or many!) and possibly return to my hometown in Mexico and give back
3. Create a non-profit that helps newly immigrated Latino students and families assimilate to this country

A LIFE OF DECISIONS

Araceli DeLeon Mendez

"Be proud of your decisions and the experiences that you will encounter."

Sometimes what you choose turns into a blessing, and sometimes it feels like a never-ending battle of self-doubt. I've had to make some very hard decisions in my lifetime and every single one has led me to where I am today.

I had a good childhood with a loving family who was able to provide everything I needed. My father is from Jalisco, Mexico and my mother is Tejano. They both worked in factories but in opposite shifts in order to provide for us. I am the oldest of three and have a younger brother and sister. My duty was to make sure my siblings had breakfast, completed their homework, and got to and from school. We spent all of our free time together and I was always responsible for them when my parents were at work. As a result, I became like a second mother to them. I felt as though they were my responsibility and I gained a habit of putting them and their needs above mine. I was always late to school because I was making sure they arrived to school on time. I was used to this routine and would sometimes forget that I was a child myself. I grew up faster than the kids around me and in a way, had my childhood stolen from me. I didn't recognize it at the time, but now that I'm older I wish I was able to participate in sports, band, and other extracurricular activities.

EARLY LESSONS

I went to East Aurora High School, which is about 40 miles outside of Chicago. It didn't have a great reputation, especially compared to our rival West Aurora High School. The graduation rate was low, and the gang activity was high. East's goal was to have their students graduate; they did not promote higher education.

As I entered my junior year, I started working. My parents always gave me the things I needed like food, shelter, and love but I still needed gas to drive my siblings to school and back. I was driving forty-five minutes across town to work at an ice cream shop. I remember being put on the schedule every weekday after school until ten or eleven o'clock in the evening. I would run the shop on my own, without a break, and this is where I learned to multi-task. I was always cleaning dishes, making ice cream, and organizing everything, all while serving customers. I did this for two and a half years until I was fired for eating too much ice cream, which I felt entitled to do because I was worked so hard. Losing that job was a small taste of how life really works; I should have stood up for myself instead.

When I graduated, I was accepted into an out-of-state university. I had applied only to see if I would get in; I didn't know much about college in general. I was still taking care of my siblings who were just entering their teenage years. I had to decide if I was going to go away to college or stay home and help with my siblings. I had reached my goal of graduating high school, so I felt if I went away to another state, I would be abandoning them. My siblings meant the world to me and I had spent most of my life as their support system. So, I decided to stay home and enroll in a community college.

My parents had suggested I work but since I got into a university, I felt I should give college a try. In my first semester, I joined Latinos Unidos, a group focused on Latinos becoming professionals and giving back to the community. I took a trip to Washington D.C. with Latinos Unidos to protest for immigration reform in early 2010, and met two students from Aurora University, David and Qoca'vib, who introduced me to a nonprofit called Family Focus.

While volunteering there, I developed some great relationships with David Blancas, Violet Flores, and Jesus Diaz. They were all working in the childhood development program which gave underprivileged students a chance to receive help with homework, life skills development, and go on educational field trips.

I worked with the middle school kids and related to them the most. I knew exactly what they were experiencing with gang influence, trying to take care of siblings, and trying to grow into young adults. I started to gain more responsibilities within the program and had to decide if I should stay in school or focus on my work.

I was proud of what I was doing and felt like I was benefitting the community. I was also able to bring my siblings along if they wanted to help with the afterschool program. Eventually, I decided to drop out of the community college and take care of my community. I did a lot of community outreach, fundraising, and volunteering with citizen workshops. I loved this job, working with kids, and helping out my community. But we all know good things come to an end. We started to lose funding, and I had to decide if I was going to stay in a job with no room for growth or start from the beginning.

HITTING THE RESTART BUTTON

I was struggling with the idea of leaving my beloved job to find something more stable. My father told me to never settle and to learn as much as I could. By this time, my brother had graduated high school and enlisted in the military. My sister was a senior and wanted to go to college. I no longer had to care for them so for the first time I was making my wants a priority. My selfish decisions caused a disagreement within my family, which led me to move in with my older cousin Andrea and her family.

This was a difficult time for me. My life had always centered around my siblings, so I didn't know where to begin. I was encouraged to go back to school to get my degree. Truthfully, I didn't know what I wanted to do so I enrolled in a trade school. I knew I needed a job and didn't believe I was ready to go back to the community college. I started a medical assisting program and was excelling. I grasped everything quickly and was excited about learning about the body and how it works.

In my free time, I was spending a lot of time with my cousin who taught me to be independent. She and her husband, John, taught me how to manage my money, manage my time, and how to persevere. They were always encouraging their kids to give their best effort and to be kind. Watching their sons grow helped me realize that I also needed to be the best version of myself, not only for me, but for them. They deserved to have a good role model, just as my cousin was a role model for me at that time. I'm proud to say I graduated at the top of my class with a 4.0.

NONSTOP DECISIONS

I've gained great knowledge working as a medical assistant for the past seven years. I started working in pediatrics for the first year out of school because I knew I loved working with children and believed it was the best place for me to be. Now, let's just say working in school with students is a completely different experience than seeing them in the doctor's office giving them their immunizations. I was no longer viewed as Ms. Araceli, the cool adult. I was now the one who children feared the most.

I also found myself in a similar situation as when I was working in the ice cream shop. I was the only one working weekends, and I was multi-tasking as the receptionist, as well as the medical assistant who was rooming patients and giving immunizations. This time I knew how to handle this situation. I asked for assistance and a raise. After waiting for three months without a change, I decided I deserved more than what I was receiving.

After leaving pediatrics, I started to work for a pain management clinic. It was a hybrid office. One side of the building was for consults and follow up appointments with the physician assistants and the other side was a surgical center in which patients received cortisone injections.

I always remembered what my father told me about being willing to learn everything. No task was too simple or too complicated for me. I've worked alongside others who said certain tasks were not part of their job descriptions, but I didn't mind the busy work. Doing those tasks showed my bosses that I was driven and flexible.

I learned how to work as a team in the operating rooms. We would have to set up the procedures for the patients, assist the doctors and also watch the patient during the entire procedure. I became very good at knowing what instruments or medicines each doctor needed at certain times of the procedure. I paid close attention to details and would always go above and beyond my job to help the patient. Sometimes patients would get a little dizzy during the injections and pass out. My job was always to assist the doctors in whatever they needed. We worked and problem-solved together, which is something I learned on the job and is not taught in textbooks.

In addition to my daily duties of rooming patients, taking

vitals, setting up the procedures and helping the nurses with post procedure patients, I learned how to order supplies and manage budgets as the ordering manager. As I grew within my role, I also started to mature. I moved into my own apartment and decided to return to school. I was working full time and going to school part time, focusing on a degree in management. I felt like everything was falling into place.

I was starting to get settled into my new routine when I met this guy. He was tall, dark, and handsome, as they all are when they sweep you off your feet. Now, I know what you're thinking—everything is going great for me, right? That's what I thought too.

He was different than my other relationships. He always put me first and for the first time in my whole life I felt like I was being taken care of, instead of the one doing the caretaking. I took care of people for a living; I had never experienced such a feeling of security before.

After dating for some time, I became pregnant. I remember the moment I found out and I cried in disbelief for days. It was a weird mixture of emotions. I was happy, I was disappointed, but overall, I was scared. I told tall, dark, and handsome and his reaction wasn't what I expected. After months of treating me like a queen, he told me flat out that he couldn't be a part of this child's life, or at least didn't want to help raise them. After that, &*^% hit the fan. I had multiple decisions that had to be made and I didn't know which way was right.

I didn't know if I should continue with the pregnancy or have an abortion. I was going to do this alone, so I needed to put my best interests first. If I had this child, would I have to quit school? Could I try to finish as much as I could before the baby was born? The outcomes were endless and I started to develop a lot of anxiety about my future.

The hardest decision of my life was made for me by fate. I was heartbroken, abandoned by my guy, and didn't have the baby. I fell into a deep depression, realizing how precious life was and also dealing with the sudden change from being pregnant and making plans, to suddenly no longer being pregnant.

My life completely changed after that. I took time off from school to focus on my well-being. My cousin Orlando, who was my roommate at the time, helped guide me through that darkness. He would tell me that I needed to put myself first and not give a damn about anyone else or what they thought. I didn't tell anyone about this time in my life except for him and my best friend, Casey, who held my hand throughout the entire thing.

She was my saving grace. Without judgment, and only kindness, she helped me decide to make the next decision in my life. Orlando taught me that I needed to be my own advocate and the one in control of my life and feelings, without anyone's opinions. Casey taught me that it's okay to be single, independent, and fearless. It was such a challenging and fragile time for me. With time, I healed, and it wasn't an overnight type of healing; it took a couple years. I was ready to focus on myself and find my happiness again.

With perseverance and dedication, I graduated with a degree in management from Waubonsee Community College. I had finally accomplished the goal I had set for myself and for the first time since my pregnancy, I was happy. I was scared of what was to come but I promised myself that I would continue on with my education and learn as much as possible.

I was 1 working in the medical field in general surgery with Northwestern Medicine, taking classes with an emphasis on public health and getting used to my routine and feeling comfortable again. Then COVID-19 hit the U.S. in the beginning of 2020 and I was exposed at work and in quarantine for two weeks.

I had to use all my paid time off (PTO) in order to get paid while at home. Once I returned to work in mid-March, my hours were cut. Since I had used up all my PTO, I was now out of work.

SERVING THOSE WITH COVID-19

I didn't know what to do or how I was going to pay my bills. I remember sitting at home and just crying. I called my manager and asked if there was anything I could do in other departments. She called around and I was placed into the labor pool. I was offered a chance to cross-train as a patient care tech. For seven years, I'd worked outpatient and didn't have any experience in the hospital. During my training there were individuals who would not help me and were unwilling to do anything outside of their realm. So I didn't know what to expect on my first day at the hospital.

I was nervous, scared, and overwhelmed to say the least when I was placed on the COVID-19 unit. My heart felt like it was dropped into my stomach that entire shift. I was working on the unit for two months. My job was to help clean patients, take their vitals, and assist them with walking/standing and checking glucose. What I didn't expect was the large Latinx population with COVID-19. There were some nights when I had eight Spanish-speaking patients. Once I arrived, the nurses and patients would call me over to help translate. Seeing people struggle with COVID-19 along with a language barrier broke my heart.

We had a strict no-visitor policy which led to all of our patients being alone for weeks at a time. I would spend my time getting to know those patients, asking about their families, and giving them my undivided attention. I was treating them with respect and kindness because they deserved it, especially in the situation they were in. COVID-19 was new and there wasn't a lot of information on treatment. Patients were fine one night, then in decline the next.

I experienced my first patient death while working the floor alone with a new nurse. We both didn't know the procedure on what to do when a patient expired. After the shift change, the nurse went home and another nurse wasn't assigned to my patient. I kept thinking about my own family and how this patient deserved better. I made the decision to take her to the morgue myself. This was one of the hardest things I've had to do. Not physically, but mentally.

I've only experienced death in my personal life, not in my professional life. They say the first death sticks with you. This is true, and I will never forget that night. Having to do postmortem care, taking the patient through the hospital to the morgue, the sadness in staff as they saw us walking the halls, and knowing she passed alone are all memories. I stuck around the COVID unit until I was needed back at my home department.

On the bright side, I learned a new role and helped out my community in a pandemic. I am now cross-trained for inpatient and outpatient settings which in the medical field, is an advantage. Although, what I learned the most is that I can handle anything thrown my way. I am proud that I stuck with it even though I was uncomfortable and intimidated by the whole situation. I always went into work with the mindset that the patient comes first, I was there to help make their stay a little more comfortable, and nothing was beyond my job description.

As you can tell, I love helping others. I had to make a few challenging decisions along the way and each one of those choices led me to exactly where I am today. Sometimes the decisions are tough and sometimes they are easy, but they all impact our lives one way or another. Be proud of your decisions and the experiences that you will encounter. I promise you, if you persevere, you will find your way, even if it's the path less chosen.

THINK YOUNG AND GROW!

My challenge to you as a reader is to stop and evaluate your life. List all the major decisions you've made in your life. Consider them and understand how the decisions you made helped get you to where you are now. Whether the decision was good, or whether it was bad, use those decisions to understand yourself. Understand that who you are today or who you want to be will be driven by your will and perseverance, guided by the decisions you make.

THIS IS ME

I am Araceli DeLeon-Mendez and I currently attend Northern Illinois University while simultaneously working full-time with Northwestern Medicine. I care deeply about people and their welfare and am deeply committed to getting people access to the healthcare they need. I enjoy learning more about the nation by seeing different cultures and meeting different people.

To become a strong role model in the medical field, especially in the Latinx community, and show that it is attainable to be a strong woman in a higher position.

THE FIVE-YEAR PLAN

1. I want to be a successful director of a hospital to ensure that people and patients are getting the best care possible.
2. Travel. Travel. Travel. Visit all 50 states.
3. Spend as much time with my parents and family as possible, exploring the world, creating memories, and learning as much as I can from them.

A CONDO DOWNTOWN

Avelira Gonzalez

"Failure is NOT an option!"

There I was in the car on the way to church on a frigid Sunday morning, bundled up with multiple scarves from the secondhand store, trying to adjust to our new city. Straight from the hot, tropical island of Puerto Rico, we had landed in the Windy City. As we drove down California Avenue, near Humboldt Park, my parents spoke about the devotional and the sermon my daddy would be preaching. My sister Tiara and I sat silently, thinking about what we would be having for lunch after service that day. As we got closer to the church, I stared into the distance and saw what I still think to be one of the most beautiful sights: the Chicago skyline. All the voices in the car became muffled and I drifted into the future.

I imagined myself sitting on the balcony of an expensive condominium, overlooking Lake Michigan on a sunny afternoon. I further imagined sitting at a desk, staring into the sunset and planning my next move. It was then that I realized that one day

I would reach my goals. I would live downtown in the hustle and bustle of the best city in the world, Chicago. However, until then, I had to make things happen!

In my house, the word "impossible" did not exist. *Papi* and *Mami* came to Chicago from our island of Puerto Rico with a dream. They forged their way through life from the ground up; Papi from a family of eight with a single mother and Mami, from a family of thirteen, an alcoholic and abusive father, and a submissive, and humiliated mother. There we were, ready to walk through our journey and conquer *El Sueño Americano* (The American Dream).

The year was 1998. The place: Arecibo, Puerto Rico. There I was, a junior at InterAmerican University at the tender age of nineteen. I received word that the President of the United States, Bill Clinton, created a grant to allow college students in the process of obtaining their bachelor's degree in English to teach English as a Second Language (ESOL) due to the shortage of English language teachers on the island. As I am bilingual and fluent in both languages and had the minimum requirement of college credits in the field, I applied. Boom! I was immediately hired to teach ELL in a second-grade classroom, full time. I was able to make the adjustments in my schedule to teach second graders English during the day and go straight to my bachelor-level classes at night, Monday through Thursday. In the wink of an eye, I became an ELL Teacher, while learning how to become a teacher. It was GREAT, and I was able to experience the best of both the academic and "real" world even before graduation. I was *open* to the opportunity, I *did not* hesitate, and I simply *acted!*

MY JOURNEY TO ADMINISTRATION

Throughout my educational journey, I have served in many different capacities. But my goal was always to become an administrator. There was something about being an administrator that seemed to call my name. I am a natural born leader, born in a household of two ordained ministers, and I taught my first Vacation Bible School (VBS) class in my early teens. I was comfortable leading others towards excellence. After teaching in Puerto Rico, I moved to the city of Boston. I served as a middle school teacher, working with students new to the country. What an amazing experience! I then served in the state of Florida, teaching as the department chair of the English Language Learner (ELL) teachers. What an opportunity to serve back to the community, teaching the language I learned years ago for the first time in the city of Chicago. I aspired to do more, to be more, to reach more.

In September of 2004, my principal pulled me aside and told me that it was time for a promotion. He had promoted a dean, which left an empty seat for me. I've always believed that if something is meant for you it is written in twenty-four karat gold and no one can take it from you, especially when it is the perfect timing of God. I believe we are all created with a purpose, with a mission in mind; not just to sit, but to act. Not just to exist, but to make a difference in someone's life. So, knowing this, I took the challenge and began my journey to become an administrator. I served as a Dean of Students, among several other positions, for five years in Florida. Little did I know that my time to reach more was on its way.

The time had come to move back to the state of Illinois. I arrived, fully certified as both an ELL teacher and administrator, from the state of Florida. However, when I arrived, I discovered that my certifications were not sufficient. I thought arriving with years of experience in teaching and administration that I was now highly qualified. During my time in Boston and Florida, I was able to obtain two master's degrees related to education. I for sure would be hired and certified right? What I didn't know was that I would be pushed to complete yet more, I learned perseverance firsthand. In order to be an administrator in Illinois, I had to take several tests and complete a third master's degree. What I didn't know was the true TEST of my values, ethics, morals, determination and grit was well underway!

KNOWING YOUR PATH

It was a Saturday morning and I woke up nice and early. I was determined and ready to take one test with five subsections. This was necessary! I needed to prove my competency, I needed to prove my grit, my determination, my passion! I was focused on being certified as an administrator in Illinois. I could've given up, gone back to teaching, packed up my family and went right back to Florida, but I didn't. I could've leaned on the fact that I had already proven to be a successful and competent administrator for years in Florida, but I didn't, I wanted more and there was a price to pay. As a parent and a professional, it was not in my plans to sign up for a third master's degree. Nonetheless, I knew my path. I gathered my children, reiterated my goals, and we prayed together before I headed out to take a four-hour test. This test would allow me to obtain my administrator's license in Illinois and keep the dean position I was hired to serve in with a waiver and condition to pass the test. Off I went, palms sweaty, heart racing, but focused. I was ready to prove that I was a competent, fourteen--year veteran educator and administrator.

So, I walked in, gave my ID to the girl at the counter, put all my things in a locker, took the test, and returned to my desk four hours later, confident that I had passed. I walked up to the counter, and the lady did not make eye contact; she simply handed me a paper from the printer, face down. I slid it in my pocket but didn't have the guts to look at it. I speed-walked to the car, eyes watering and heart fluttering. I unlocked the door and sat in my car in silence. I took a deep breath, and with my right hand shaking, I took the paper out of my pocket. I could hear my breathing becoming shallow and ragged. I counted backwards from ten, and when I reached one, I turned the paper around… and BOOM! I saw a word that would become my new norm… FAILED in capital letters, bold and italicized to add insult to injury. What am I going to tell my kids when I got home? I wondered. How will I tell HR on Monday? What do I tell my family that has been praying for me to pass with flying colors? After fourteen years of successful evaluations as a teacher and an administrator, how do I fail a test? I can run a school, but I can't pass a test?

THE MAGIC NUMBER

It was another Saturday morning and my routine was now automatic. With coffee in hand, I meet with the kiddos before heading out to take the test, this time, for the twentieth time. You read correctly, I had taken and failed the same test, twenty times in the span of two years. This time, I had attended reviews of the test, spoken to colleagues that passed it, and prayed. I didn't lose hope; I had cried, the ugly kind where slime drips down past your lips and down your neck. I knew that my destiny was to continue being an administrator. I knew I was cut from cloth that made me determined and persistent; giving up was not in my DNA. So, in I went.

Four hours later, I received the paper, once again, face down. I walked to my car, turned the paper around and for the twentieth time, the six-letter word stared me in the face… FAILED! My world once again crumbled. How is it that I can't get this right? It took one more try… the magic number, twenty-one. Twenty-one mornings, twenty-one registration fees of one hundred dollars. Repeated time and effort, again and again. I excelled in other areas but couldn't jump this hurdle. It was time to explore another way for me to prove competency.

In conversation with the State, I was able to provide the scores of my high school SAT scores from over sixteen years ago which held the key for me to prove competency and finally earn my administrative license in the State of Illinois. Nearly five years later, I was able to obtain and reach my goal. A test didn't define my talents, nor my capabilities and ability to lead with a purpose.

I am currently an Assistant Principal for Student Services and am completing my superintendent endorsement in the state of Illinois.

THINK YOUNG AND GROW

I invite you to reflect upon the lessons I learned in my journey by answering the following questions:

1. **Where do you come from?** Never forget where you come from, what legacy you are creating, and what is written in twenty-four karat gold for you that cannot be taken away or erased.
2. **Where are you going?** Begin with your final destination in mind, stay focused and continue pushing.
3. **Drilling holes or rowing?** Make sure that the people in your boat are rowing and not drilling holes. Identify the voices that surround you, silence those that are drilling holes and kindly ask them to get off the boat. Focus on the ones that are rowing with you towards your final destination.

Failure is not an option; it is time to obtain the skills, resources, and information that sets you up for a successful and productive life. Zero excuses!

THIS IS ME

Raised in the city of Chicago, born on the beautiful island of Puerto Rico, I have served as an educator and administrator for twenty-two years in a diversity of settings. My passion is music and education. I am a single mother of two wonderfully talented children and education is my priority. I have completed three master's degrees and throughout my career, I have served as a teacher of English as a Second Language (ESL), and as a human resources manager and school administrator.

I came from a home where my mother completed a sixth-grade education and finally earned her bachelor's degree and my father completed several doctorates and a master's degree at Harvard University. I am proud that they too have excelled, despite their environment.

To become the first Latina superintendent of a diverse high school district.

THE FIVE-YEAR PLAN

1. Earn my doctoral degree in educational leadership
2. Own a house
3. Become the first Latina superintendent of a diverse high school district

EMBRACING ME

Brenda Hernandez

"Whatever you are the 'first' to do, you are not alone."

I was very blessed to have grown up in a town with a lot of diversity. I was never the only Latina in my school or the only minority in my classroom. I had best friends that were Latinx, Black and White. I was exposed to many different backgrounds —from kids who had siblings in gangs and were raised in single parent, low-income homes, to children whose parents had their own business or who both parents had gone to college. Growing up, I never paid much attention to any of those things or looked closely at my own skin color or background. My mom always told me not to share too much about my life since my siblings and I weren't born in the U.S., so I didn't. It was hard for me to embrace myself fully because I felt like I couldn't share all of me with the world. I now hope to change that.

A NEW WORLD

My life changed the moment I saw the smallest pieces of

white-colored, cotton candy fall from the sky. It was my first time seeing snow. My mom, dad, two elder brothers, younger sister and I had just spent three days on a bus from Mexico to arrive at our new home. In those three days, my horizons changed from green mountains, to dirt roads, busy streets, tall buildings, and towards the end of the trip, sad, dead grass.

It was January 1, 2004. Outside the bus, the sky was colorless, as if someone forgot to paint it blue, and there was a sense of stillness. When I stepped out of the bus, I was welcomed by frigid air that entered my lungs and created a shiver that ran through my small, seven-year-old body. Things felt, looked, and smelled differently than home. I knew this was the place my mom and dad wanted to raise their four children so they could learn the language and get an education. This was the land of dreams everyone talked about, and now it was my new home. This was the United States.

Life in the U.S. was clearly different than life in Mexico. I entered first grade a shy, skinny, little brown girl who didn't know any English. I didn't even know how to open up the milk cartons we were given for our school breakfast and didn't know how to ask for help. I could tell that the other kids looked at me a little strangely because I didn't speak English and dressed differently. That made my first year in elementary school a little lonely, but thankfully I could always go back home and play with my two brothers and sister. I knew I wasn't alone in this new land.

Luckily, six months into our move, I was able to learn English, but even when I did, I still felt like I stuck out and not in a good way. As I started getting a little older, I began noticing that I didn't dress like the other girls or have nice clothes. Instead, I would wear hand-me-downs from my older brothers and the kids at school noticed and made fun of me. That's when I first realized that my family's circumstances weren't extremely common. I thought it was normal for a family of six to live in a two-bedroom apartment, for me to share a room with three siblings, and for our parents not to speak English. I hadn't found it odd to wear my older brother's hand me down sweatpants to school or wear the same shirt two times in a row because I didn't have enough clothes, or that for a few years our only Christmas presents had been from church donation programs for low-income families.

Realizing this at my age made me very insecure. I remembered my mom's advice when we first moved to the U.S.: "Don't share too much about yourself." So I didn't. I figured the best way to make it through school and mean kids was to make myself as invisible as possible so nobody would notice me or the things I lacked. I tried embracing who I was, but something inside me made me feel uneasy, like I didn't belong.

As I entered middle school, I decided to try the whole "fitting in" thing. I decided to become one of those cool girls all the boys wanted, who skipped classes, got bad grades, played sports, and had lots of friends. I achieved every step except two crucial ones: boys and lots of friends. Early in eighth grade, I decided being "popular" or "fitting in" wasn't for me. It was a lot of work trying to go with the flow of the crowd, plus, I discovered that most "popular" girls were fueled by drama, and I knew I did not want that. I chose to do really well in school instead, since fitting in didn't get me anywhere and good grades got me good notes from my teachers. I started to get placed into "advanced" classes for "smart" students. In those classes, popularity wasn't about who had the nicest clothes; it was about the kids who got one hundred or ninety percent on their tests.

I entered high school with one goal in mind: do the best I could, academically. I saw that my efforts in school were paying off, so I wanted to continue. Also, at that time, I had a boyfriend who I had started dating at the end of middle school. I didn't know it then, but I would be in a relationship with him for almost five years, and it would be a blessing in disguise. He was an extremely jealous guy, so outside of our relationship and school, I didn't have many friends and I used that time to put extra effort into my schoolwork. As I mentioned, it was a blessing in disguise because I was able to laser-focus on my studies. He caused me a lot of emotional pain, but sometimes it's the situations that bring you heartbreak and tears that build the foundation of strength for later in life.

MY PLAN

In my freshman year of high school, school counselors started to mention college. I didn't personally know anyone who was in college or who had attended college, so I had no idea how to apply, the requirements, how to pay for it, or if college life was really like it was portrayed in movies. Since I was in the "advanced" classes where students talked about their next step after high school being college, I started to think that was just the next stepping stone after graduation. Sort of like how you move from elementary school to middle school, then high school. I decided I wanted this too. I knew my parents came to the U.S to better our education. I knew that in Mexico, in the town I'm from, most girls only attend middle school, maybe high school and rarely college. To me, attending college meant that my parents leaving their family behind and resettling here was all worthwhile. It was then that I decided my plan: attend college. I started to join different clubs like the school newspaper, and I was part of the National Honor Society, did sports like soccer, cross country, and track, and volunteered in different places. I knew that colleges didn't only like good students with good grades, but students who were leaders involved in their school. Besides, all of the kids who talked about college were doing this too so I knew my efforts wouldn't go to waste.

As high school was coming to an end, I realized my dreams of attending college would be much harder than expected. I was having a conversation with my dad and revealed to him my deep desire to go to college and receive the college experience everyone talked about. He responded "Well, good luck with your dreams because I am not going to help you. Get there yourself." I was shocked because I wasn't expecting my parent's financial support, but I was expecting them to support my decision. "If you can't go to school, you should just get a job," he said. A job? After 12 years in school I didn't want a job right away. My oldest brother, Jamer, had gone to college after high school and my brother, Jonathan, decided to work. I looked up to them both for being the first in our families to do either because as I mentioned, to graduate high school is a great accomplishment back home. I had two examples I could follow, and I decided for me, I wanted college. I later told my mom about my dad's attitude. *"Mira, tu sigue adelante"* she said, which roughly translates to "keep moving forward." She was right. I decided that I didn't care how I was going to do it, but I was going to go to college and somehow pay for it.

I'm a big believer in experiencing different things, and thankfully, I followed my own advice, because the summer of my high school junior year, I decided I would try running cross country and found a hidden talent: I could run.

The first year I gave running a try, I always came in last. I was running in Jordans, which were basketball shoes, and very heavy. I eventually bought some running shoes and made a training plan for myself based on what I researched the best runners were doing. I dove into training, and by senior year, I was one of the best runners in my state. Colleges throughout Wisconsin began to notice me, and this brought me into a whole new world that I didn't know about. I was getting scholarship offers to attend school and run!

All the hard work I put into my years of studies in high school paid off because I was able to apply and interview for a prestigious, full-ride scholarship that would pay for all four years of my education. I got the phone call while I was away at a track meet, and when I got home, my mom told me the news. Of course, I couldn't believe it! How did that happen? Shortly after, I got a phone call from one of the universities I visited for a potential opportunity to attend, and they offered me an athletic scholarship! My dream to attend college became a reality.

A NEW LENSE

College was not what I expected. Freshman year was emotional. Even though I wasn't too far from home, the adjustment of seeing my family every day, to only once a month, was difficult. I parted ways with the boyfriend I had since middle school, and I was also part of a Division 1 athletic team, and that was nerve-wracking. On the cross-country team, I felt like the black sheep of the bunch—or brown sheep, I should say. Most of my teammates were White, came from small towns, or attended schools without a lot of minorities. This was when I really started to take notice of my own skin. My tan skin was very different from nearly all of my teammates. At one point I was told by one of them that I talked "funny." Apparently, they hadn't spoken to many people who had accents.

The feeling was similar to the one I had back when I first moved to the U.S., that feeling of not belonging. It didn't sit well with me, so I decided to search for new connections elsewhere. At that point, I was starting college on a completely new slate. I was in a new city and figured, why not take chances? I joined different organizations and started to meet people from different backgrounds, experiences, perspectives and even people who looked like me! Through one of those organizations, I met a confident, cool guy named Carlos Sierra. We hit it off in the beginning by becoming friends through our love of real human conversations and similar backgrounds. I admired the way he looked at life. He wanted to change the world, and I shared a similar dream.

When I first started college, I wanted to go into the medical field. My eldest brother, Jamer, is a nurse and I wanted to follow in his footsteps, but after two years of atoms and body systems, I knew that science wasn't for me. Carlos, who at that point had developed into my crush, encouraged me to take a look at the business school. He thought I was outgoing, and my personality would allow me to do well in roles facing people. Changing into a business major pushed me to get involved even more as I learned that internships were a must in order to start a good career after college.

Through my involvement in different organizations and by being a student athlete, I was exposed to countless opportunities. I was able to travel to compete in different states for track and cross country, I was able to meet incredible people who mentored me in different areas of my life, and gain career experience that enabled me to get internships. I had broken out of my shell, but through those experiences, I also felt something was missing. Even though I navigated many different situations, meeting different people, I still was not embracing myself fully. In the different spaces, there were often very few others who looked like me. Where were all the other Latinas who had backgrounds like mine? Who understood the struggle of being the only one that looks like you in the room? Who understood that I couldn't go home and talk to my parents about my career moves because they didn't fully understand the space I was in? It took a while for me to notice that this was the missing piece of the puzzle: it was the constant, internal battle between embracing myself and wanting to be surrounded by others like me.

I hit an all-time low at the end of my second to last semester. I was done with my running eligibility, so I had a lot more time to focus on getting ready to take the next step in my life, which was my first job out of college. I felt so lost and unsure of what I wanted and questioned myself constantly. I wondered if in the next step of my life, I would again have the feeling of not fitting in. A semester later, and shortly after graduating, sure enough, I realized that I was one of the only Latinas in the role I was in.

Sometime during that time, I took a chance and decided to attend a book launch in Chicago. After a three-hour drive down to the event, I arrived at a room filled with many inspirational Latina women. I was in complete awe. I felt inspired and like I truly belonged. I personally thank God for placing me there because it gave me that lift of hope I needed at a time where I felt discouraged. After that event, I understood the quote by Helen Keller: "Alone we can do so little, together we can do so much." Together, united as force, we can make a change.

NEW HOPE

The event sparked in me the hope that I can help bring Latinas into places we are underrepresented. I know for me the support of my high school coach, Coach Shaver, empowered me to take that next leap in my life. Without his support, it would have been extremely difficult for me to figure out how to attend college and become a student athlete. I understand that others are not as fortunate, so I feel it is my obligation to offer help when I can. My hope is to inspire any young girl or woman reading this to embrace the space they are in. Usually as women, especially as Latinas, we are put into situations where we are the first to do something in our families. Whatever you are the "first" to do, whether it's the first to go to school, or get a job right out of high school, or start a business, you are not alone. I often felt alone and lost because I felt I couldn't share my feelings, and nobody would understand. I now know that isn't true. By reading this book you can see that you are not alone. I know that my journey is unique, and my little sister Yasmin will also have her own journey too, and her journey will differ from that of her friends and so on. You are where you are meant to be and in whatever you are doing, you have the endless support of others who look like you and who are silently cheering you on because they know what it feels like to be alone, or scared to do it all wrong.

It took me twenty-three years to fully embrace myself—my beautiful tan skin, my accent, my upbringing, my awkwardness, my interests and my position and roles. Embracing me is a work in progress, and some days I'm stronger than others. Regardless, I aim to embrace all of me completely because I know that somewhere out there, there is a young Latina girl questioning why she doesn't fit in, look like others, or talk like others. I would hope that if she and I ever cross paths, that she will see me loving and being myself fully, and know that if I can do it, she can do it too.

THINK YOUNG AND GROW

I encourage you to get a journal and write. Writing helps you reflect and liberate you from any thoughts that might be constantly running around in your mind. Through journaling you will learn about who you are and what you stand for. Journaling also helps you reflect back on what brought you tears and smiles. Sometimes when we are in the moment, our emotions can take over. Journaling can help you reflect on those moments. Another huge tip into starting anything: jump right in! Take the action towards anything you want. Planning and thinking about doing something will keep you in the same spot you are in. Who you are today is the result of the actions you did or did not take in the past few months. Who you will be tomorrow, and the months to follow, will be a result of what you choose to do today.

THIS IS ME

I am a twenty-three-year-old, powerful Latina woman learning through life's experiences. Born in Guanajuato, Mexico, I moved to Wisconsin at the age of seven. My values and personality stem from my two older brothers, my little sister, my two four-legged furry friends, and my wonderful parents. I attended the University of Wisconsin-Milwaukee, where I ran Division 1 Cross Country and Track, and graduated with my bachelor's degree in marketing with a finance emphasis. Currently, I work in sales at a top tech company and plan to continue developing my sales and business skills by learning from the best. Outside of work, you can find me reading personal development books, getting lost in YouTube videos, dancing bachata, and enjoying time with my boyfriend, Carlos, my lovely family, and beautiful friends.

My dream is to be part of a TV show series or movie and grow the diversity of Latinas in the media.

THE FIVE-YEAR PLAN

1. Launch a consistent, biweekly blog where I can share different experiences about life and share tips.
2. Start my own business and invest in real estate and move down to a sunny state with no winters.
3. Audition to become part of a short film or tv series.

LOVING MYSELF SO I CAN LOVE OTHERS

Crystal Alina Prusek

"I have to be my own biggest advocate."

In May 2019, I found myself crossing the street, feeling a little cautious but hopeful that I might find some help. I was walking into my first Queer group grief counseling session. It was a group specifically for those who had lost a loved one.

Before going in, I was feeling stuck in a cycle of unhappiness where I wasn't feeling hungry often, I found showering tedious, I was sleeping a lot, and feeling extremely irritable. Because of this, my partner and I went through a breakup. We were together for three years and were living together. While I tried to work out all my unhappiness, I was experiencing the harsh reality of having to separate our household items and lives.

I finally started to see that I needed to realize my worth. I admitted to myself that something had to change. I reached out to see if some type of counseling might help. I had dismissed this option before because I thought other people had it worse than me. I thought I would be able to get over it and move on. But more and more I realized I wasn't getting on with life because of my thoughts and negative self-talk. I would say things to myself like, "Your family is embarrassed of you because you haven't pursued acting after graduation," and, "You're never going to make enough money to get out of this pool of student loan debt." For some reason, I couldn't muster up the energy to get off the couch and out of my house.

LIFE WITH ALCOHOL

Six years ago, when I was eighteen, my dad passed away after a long struggle with alcoholism. My first memory of his drinking was when I was in elementary school. I walked in on him chugging beers in the garage before he left for work. Many times, I remember hearing him get sick in the bathroom after a family party and asking my mom what was wrong. I knew he took multiple shots of vodka at home after work and would always have a beer or two with dinner but I thought it was normal. I was young and assumed that adults drink when they get home from work.

What I didn't know back then was that my dad was what most would call a "functioning alcoholic," meaning he hid his drinking well, he was able to maintain relationships with the family, and hold down his job while exhibiting signs of alcoholism. With the knowledge I now have about his drinking, I can assume that anytime we were at home as a family he was drunk in some capacity.

My dad played a hands-on role with my brother and I in our childhoods. He coached me in softball from when I was five until I was fifteen and did the same for my brother, who is four years younger than me. He was always there for us and seemed like the ultimate dad.

He did sometimes lose his temper and would yell and slam doors. He worked hard to hide his alcoholism from us because once I finally realized the severity of his drinking and that he had an addiction, my parents were already getting a divorce. I was sixteen years old and my little brother was twelve.

When my parents told my brother and I that they were splitting up, I sided with my dad because I thought my mom just didn't love him anymore. That's how much I didn't know. My parents had my brother and I live in our family home full time while they switched off staying with us every couple of days. When they switched off, I was noticing a change in my dad. When he was with us, he was mostly sleeping and not taking the time to cook. He would go on about how much he missed my mom and how the divorce was all her idea.

One day, my dad was found lying outside of his car by the police after he hit his head on the curb. After that episode, he started to get progressively sicker every time I saw him. Finally, my mom cut off all contact with him. After that, my dad was no longer able to watch my brother and I on his own.

Eventually, I saw my dad's car parked outside of some strip malls near our house for days. I started to realize that he was sleeping and living in his car. My brother and my mom started to lose contact with him, but I tried to make time for him. He'd call me to vent, and I'd bring him food. I even went to Alcoholics Anonymous meetings with him. There were times that I knew he was drunk, but I just wanted to hang out and be around my dad.

Everything was going as well as it could be until the day of my high school graduation. I had planned on picking my dad up from the train station to take him with me where he could meet up with the rest of my family. While I was on my way, I got a call from his cell phone number.

"Is this Crystal?" an officer on the other end of the line asked. I braced myself for the worst.

The police explained that my dad was found drunk outside of a grocery store and they would have to take him into custody to sober up. My heart sank as I drove myself to graduation without him. I felt stupid because I was always there when he needed me, but he couldn't do the same for me. I realized that this was the reason my mom and brother cut off contact with him; they were trying to protect themselves from getting hurt. I felt embarrassed that I could be foolish enough to open myself up to getting hurt like this and not just by anyone, but my own dad. I purposefully invited him to my graduation when everyone else thought it wasn't a good idea. I thought he could prove to everyone that he was trying to heal and work through his alcoholism.

After I received the call from the police, I couldn't help but wonder if my family was right. If you don't expect anything from him, you won't get hurt when he does something disappointing. So after that, I decided I had to keep my distance so I couldn't be hurt or embarrassed like that again.

After graduation, I enrolled in Millikin University to study acting. The school is located in central Illinois about three hours away from Chicago. I stayed on campus and the change of scenery and getting the chance to be away from my family for a little while finally made me feel like I wasn't defined by my dad's addiction. Everything was going really well! I hate to say it, but I felt free because I didn't have to parent my own parent anymore. At least not in a hands-on way.

Then, in my second semester of my freshman year of college, I got the news that my dad was found dead in his car. I was in shock that it happened but unfortunately, we saw it coming. I was relieved that he wasn't suffering anymore. I just wished he could have broken his addiction, not just for us, but for himself. What I didn't expect was the pain that came afterwards and the emotional trouble I would have to experience from not facing my grief.

FROM NEGATIVE TO POSITIVE

I spent the next three years distracting myself in college with schoolwork, parties, and girlfriends. My grades were great, I loved acting, and I felt like I finally found a place where I could be myself. I craved the discipline of being asked to achieve a goal and delivering a stellar performance for my peers. Overall, I was doing the best I could after a big loss. The problem started to surface again after I graduated from college, when the afterglow of my achievement started to fade away.

I was finding it really difficult to come to terms with the

fact that my dad was gone forever. I felt like I was changing and growing, but I was growing away from the memory of my dad. He would be frozen in time, while I grew older and changed. I'd find myself wanting to share exciting news with him, then remembering that he was gone. I pushed my grief aside for so long that it would bubble over at times, manifesting itself as anxiety, anger, and stress.

It took me a long time to realize that the trauma of my dad's death was causing me to mistreat my loved ones and even myself. For example, I was harboring some inner animosity towards my mom, which manifested itself in my short temper. I knew it wasn't her fault that my dad had succumbed to his addiction; I think the child somewhere inside me was hurt by the divorce and resented that my mom ended their relationship. I was constantly angry and wanted things to go exactly as I planned. If that didn't happen, I would simply get frustrated for no reason. In general, I was losing empathy for the feelings of those around me. On top of that, I started forming my own bad habits like sleeping through the day, not eating enough, and overdrinking because I felt unworthy of being happy.

After the break-up with my ex, I was spending lots of time alone. I realized that I was generally doing things that made me unhappy and I was not heading down a path in my life that fulfilled me. I was sharing my thoughts with my mom and some friends, and everyone was telling me that therapy and introspection might be helpful in moving forward. I wanted to move on and get out of the slump I was in, and the only person who could help me was me.

After the break-up, I talked to my mom and other close friends about what I could do to turn my life around. Slowly, it started to dawn on me that I can be happy, and I deserve it too. The advice I got from the people who care about me was to seek out a therapist. After doing some research online, I found a great mental health group for people in the Queer community called Howard Brown. I managed to get up and out of my apartment and with courage and perseverance, I found myself in front of a counselor's office.

The group grief counseling sessions helped me to heal a lot. It was comfortable to be around others who had lost loved ones and to have a place to talk about that instead of feeling the pity from others as "the girl who lost her dad." I still go to group counseling for drop-in sessions but have moved closer to one-on-one therapy sessions. Even if I don't feel like I need it, I try to go at least once a month to check in on my mental health.

It was a slow roll at first, wondering if counseling was "working." How would I know if it was? At first, I was focusing on the fact that if I got "better," my girlfriend might want to take me back. Then I understood that I had to emotionally heal for myself. I learned that if I want to feel joy in life, I have to create it myself for myself. After all, no one will ever be "down" for me like I'll be "down" for myself. Yes, I have loved ones to lean on, but I have to be my own biggest advocate. I realized this and started trucking forward.

I stopped hoping that going to counseling would mend the broken relationship between my me and my ex. I started biking more and staying active, and I went to the doctor who prescribed me antidepressants to kick-start my healing process. I progressed with a positive attitude and thought process. I reminded myself that I deserved to be happy. I found a new roommate and started working on small crafting projects that brought me joy.

Once I started moving through life with a positive outlook, opportunities started opening up. I participated in some acting projects and a couple months later, I was able to meld my love for building and design with theatre. I was asked to be the set designer for a children's theater. I'm still taking medication and going to solo counseling without any stigma, because I'll always be a work in progress. I do owe a lot to my family and those close to me who I can rely on to let me know if I am falling back into bad habits or depressive cycles. My goal for now is to do things that make me happy and to keep moving forward in life.

As I was learning to love myself and trying to find my worth, I decided to try dating. I didn't want to rely on anyone to automatically bring me happiness just because of their presence in my life. Instead, I really wanted to focus on sharing my happiness and moving forward with a partner who is motivated to do the same. I stayed open and have since found a wonderful, emotionally intelligent partner who I adore! Our partnership feels equal. She helps remind me when I'm exhibiting self-sabotaging behavior or when I'm getting stuck in the house for too long. It makes me feel fulfilled because I can help her too, whether it's with my knowledge of handy tool stuff like taking apart a bed or reminding her to breathe when things start to get stressful. It's so fulfilling to be in a relationship where we communicate and help each other because we love each other, not because we want to change each other.

Through all of this, I've realized the importance of acknowledging your trauma. It's not that you're acknowledging your trauma to get stuck in the "would've, could've, should've." Instead, it's to move past it, because the memory is always there. You should acknowledge the trauma so that you can live with it, see how it makes you unique and stronger, and use it as your superpower.

I'll never forget the pain of losing my dad. Even though I miss him, and our life together became very difficult at times, I can credit him with helping me create the productive, vibrant, truly happy life I have at the moment. My goal now is just to keep feeling more confident about what I have to offer the world, treating myself with kindness, and enjoying this amazing life that I have. I still go to therapy at least two times a month and I take antidepressants. Overall, I think I'm a work in progress, like everyone, but ultimately if I hadn't taken those first steps of going to talk to a therapist, who knows where I would be now?

THINK YOUNG AND GROW!

I'd like to challenge you to create a "Gratitude Journal." Set aside a little bit of time each day to write down things that you're grateful for. It can be anything from your fingernail to your car. This will help you remember the things that really matter in life and keep out the intrusive negative self-talk that sometimes happens.

Another challenge is to try some power poses. Power poses are big open poses. For example, standing with your legs apart, hands on your hips, and holding your chin up, like a superhero. Hold your pose for a few minutes while remembering to breathe in through your nose and out through your mouth. Smiling during this exercise, or anytime you're feeling overwhelmed, will help you to "fake it till you make it."

The last challenge is to change "sorry's" to "thank you's." Instead of saying something like, "sorry I was late," you could say something like "thank you for being so patient." This will help you stop apologizing for your existence and help you appreciate those around you for being there.

THIS IS ME

My name is Crystal Alina Prusek and I live in Chicago with my partner, Jordan, and our three cats. I graduated from Millikin University in 2017 with a BFA in Acting. I did set design for Greenhouse Children's theater for their 2019 production of West Side Story. I'm currently working on getting accepted to a coding boot camp to start my career as a software engineer. I'm hoping that as a software engineer, I will find a way to contribute to projects close to my heart in the visual and performing arts. In the meantime, I love to do woodworking. I've built my own dining room table, shelves, pot and pan holder, and bridges for my cats to hang out on the walls. In short, I love to build, travel, and be a part of things that make me happy.

Marry my current partner and have a family, working remotely as a software engineer, participating in the dance world in Chicago or trying my hand at film acting.

THE FIVE-YEAR PLAN

1. Have enough money saved to begin build my own sustainable, "Tiny House"
2. Become financially stable to pay off my student debt and help my mom
3. Create a safe art space for people in the Queer community

MI VERDAD

Miriam Bigurra

"I can't let negative things come to me."

I stood there singing my heart out while Fer, from the rock group Mana, held my hand and I felt like never before. Fittingly, the name of the song was *Mi Verdad*, (my truth). My dream was finally coming true. I knew then and there what I wanted to do with my life.

LEGACY OF SUCCESS

Growing up, my parents always spoke about both sides of the family and what they accomplished in life. It was a way to teach my sister and me how far we could go and what we could do in life if we worked as hard as they did.

I always knew my dad's family was somewhat artistic. My grandpa is a pastor and would play the organ at church and lead the singing. My aunt sings opera and leads the church choir. On my mom's side of the family, I knew that all the women were strong and educated. In fact, my great-grandma convinced her father that she needed to go to college and be a professional, rather than be a typical housewife. She was one of the first women to wear pants in Bolivia.

My parents always told their daughters that they came to this country for a better life. My mother left Bolivia when she was about eighteen years old with her siblings, my grandparents, and great-grandparents. She always tells me that coming to the U.S. was a new beginning and a chance to become independent and live on her own. She went to Colombia College and worked two jobs to pay for school and expenses.

My dad came to the U.S. to learn English for six months and return to Mexico, but he met my mom so his plans changed and he decided to stay. He worked hard to pay for the English classes he took as well as the certifications he needed to work in the U.S.

Both the stories of my parents and their families had taught me a lot and made me who I am today. I knew that my family had worked very hard to be someone here in the U.S. just as their family had worked hard to be someone in their own country. So, I had to push myself to become someone great as well.

When I was very little, my mom put in dance classes because she loved dancing and thought I would probably enjoy it like her. I only lasted three years in dance, then I got bored, and found I preferred sports over dancing. So, my mom took my sister and I to the park district to register us to play a sport, and I told her immediately that I wanted to play soccer. I remember seeing soccer games with my family and felt like only the men played it. I needed to show that girls could play soccer too.

I played soccer for about twelve years, and even now I still play for fun with friends. Soccer was not my only passion; performing became a big passion for me too. In third grade, I auditioned for the school choir. I didn't think I would make it since I really didn't have any background in music other than playing piano. Well, to my surprise, when they posted the roster, I was on the list. Then and there I realized I had talent and that I could do more with it.

My mom put me in voice lessons, and even though I did not enjoy it when I was younger, I got back into dance lessons. When I entered junior high, I decided to audition for the school musical since I sang and danced. I was cast in it, and after that show, I enjoyed acting as well.

So my mom found acting activities and classes at the Metropolis Performing Art Center in Arlington Heights, Illinois. The more I sang, acted, and danced, the more I started to see what I wanted to be in the future. I went on to high school and I was ready to audition for the musical. I was sure I was going to get in since I was considered a triple threat. Well, I was wrong.

FINDING MY VOICE

That was the first year I was not cast in a musical or a show. *What did I do wrong?* I thought. Am I not really good at performing? What is it? I did not know what to think. My mom always said to ask the teachers for feedback to learn where I needed to improve, but I never got around to it because I was too shy to ask. So I decided to somehow still get involved in theatre and I become part of the makeup and costume crew. It was fun and I learned new things, but it was hard seeing the performers practice and not be on stage with them.

Finally, my sophomore year arrived and I was preparing myself for the musical auditions. I hoped and prayed to get in this time. I also made sure to "put myself out there" so the teachers in the theatre department knew who I was.

I put my whole heart into that audition, and luckily, I made it. I was so happy! I felt like finally I knew I was great! From then on, I was involved in the school musical sophomore through senior year. I always played a chorus part, never a lead role, which always had me thinking, *why is that?* It was hard for me to understand why I never got an actual character role in the musicals. I would start to think that maybe I was not such a good actor, singer, or dancer. People would tell me I was good and to keep practicing and I would get better and better. The insecurity of whether or not I was good enough to someday play an actual character role led me to decide what major I would study in college.

I knew I wanted to attend Columbia College in downtown Chicago, whether I studied music, dance, musical theatre, or just acting. When I started my first semester at Columbia, my major was musical theatre but within the first month, I decided to switch to acting with a minor in music. I changed my major because I felt that I would not be good enough in musical theatre and maybe if I just focused on only acting as a major and still had music as a minor, I would have an opportunity with one or the other.

My first year of school was amazing. I met new friends, and I started to find myself. I learned what I really loved and wanted to do, but not until the end of my first year. Before that, I focused a lot on having fun and meeting people, and I did not focus enough on my studies. My first semester, I felt a bit insecure about my career path since I never felt like I had enough talent during high school. Eventually, I started to audition for performing events and let others get to know me at school. People were very supportive, and I started to feel more secure than I did when I first started the program.

However, my second year of college I ended up on academic probation. I had to go to a community college to raise my GPA and prove my ability to succeed at Columbia.

It was very hard for me to accept that I had failed, but I pushed myself and worked hard. I went to Truman College for my second year and did all I could to get better grades and raise my GPA. I did very well that year and was able to return to Columbia for my third year. I had a lot of support from my family, friends, and boyfriend. They all helped me get through and motivated me to do well.

When I returned for my third year, I decided to stick only with acting as a major and no longer minor in music. Since it had been two years since I last danced, I didn't think I would be good enough to do a major in musical theatre. I still focused on my music on the side and would perform at events at school and even audition for some musicals. I ended up having to take a year and half longer than the traditional four-year path since I got behind my first year. I was able to walk at my school's graduation, but I have not been able to finish. The plan was to be done the fall semester after I walked, which was fall 2016, but things changed that year for me and led me pause my progress towards my degree.

THE SONG

In the summer of 2015, I got engaged to my boyfriend, Aroldo, right before starting my last year of school. I was so happy, and we had agreed to wait two years for the wedding so that I could finish my degree. Well, a year passed, and I focused on finishing as many credits as I could, but I still had a few left which I intended to complete in the fall semester.

Aroldo and I were doing great, and I felt he supported me through everything. Then in the summer of 2016, things started to go downhill to the point that we decided to end the relationship. That was one of the worst things that has ever happened to me, especially because he was my first boyfriend and I did not know how to handle a breakup.

I tried taking a few classes in the fall, but it became difficult for me to focus. Not only did I lose the person I loved, but in the middle of my semester, I ended up losing my dog. He got run over by a car and suffered internal injuries. I ended up having to put him to sleep. I felt a lot of pain during that time, but I worked through it and focused on finishing my semester. It was really hard, and I couldn't help but worry what other bad things could possibly happen to me.

Then, a great opportunity landed right at my feet. I got a call that changed my life and lifted my confidence and energy. I was home when the phone started to ring, and at first I didn't bother to answer since I didn't recognize the number. Then, the same caller called again, so I answered and it was the radio station 103.1, now known as 93.5. They called to give me some news and asked me to stay on the line and wait until they came back so they could tell me live on the air. So I was wondering if it was tickets, money, a prize of some sort, but I didn't know.

Well, once they went live, they announced that I was going to the Mana concert on October 22, 2016 but that I was not only going to get front row seat tickets, but I was also going to get the opportunity to sing *Mi Verdad* with them live. I started to cry, and I could not believe what they were telling me. I was in complete shock and so emotional. I actually didn't remember that a few months before, I had received a call after an audition I did for a music show and the producers asked if they could enter a video recording of me singing *Mi Verdad* in the radio station's contest. I had given them permission, but I didn't realize that the contest was for the opportunity to sing live onstage with Mana!

Immediately after that call, I started to practice. I would ask my most musical friends to help me out and I did everything I could to be ready. I had exactly three weeks to prepare.

The day came and I was full of emotions. I felt nervous and

ready, but at the same time, I was feeling the what ifs. I arrived for my sound check and practiced there until I felt I was good with my sound. Then, I just waited until the time came.

I was backstage for the beginning of the concert, and it was amazing. I could not stop feeling excited. I wanted to scream for joy, but I had to relax my voice so it would be good for my performance. I was up after the fourth or fifth song, and once they called me to be ready, I prayed and told myself it was time, and that I could do it and God would be there for me.

I walked onto the stage and it was emotional to see the Allstate arena full of people, and then, to be on stage with Mana. One of the group members, Fer, presented me and the song started. I thought I might mess up because of the all the people there, but thanks to the lights, I only was able to see the first three rows and it helped calm my nerves.

It was an amazing experience. Right at the moment, I felt everything come to me and I just thought, this is it, I *can't quit, I can't let negative things come to me, I need to keep going and push myself.*

A GREAT FUTURE

After everything negative that happened to me, having such a great opportunity before the end of 2016 was transformative. I made a promise to myself to start doing new things and focus on me.

When the New Year began, I had to fulfill my promise. I occasionally would think about my past, but I pushed myself through it. I started to go out again with some friends from school. I ended up focusing on my music and basically, focusing on me.

As time went by, I felt more confident than ever and more positive too. I started to express myself more and practice my music and acting. I did do a show and some singing, but for 2018, I put a pause on my career to focus on saving money and accomplishing some goals.

That summer, my Aroldo came back into my life and we decided to start again and get married. Things were different, and we had changed for the better. It was a new beginning, and we were going to be great. Aroldo is my biggest support, and he pushes me every day to find opportunities and be a better person.

For the moment, I have not focused much on my career since we are saving money, but I do practice my music and some monologues, so when I return to the stage, I'm ready. I also plan to get back to school and finish the last two courses I need to graduate and get a job in an artistic field.

I am proud of how far I have come in my life and the positive changes I have made in my life. I can't wait for the future!

THINK YOUNG AND GROW

We all have times where we get stuck on a decision, figuring out a plan or even just getting through a hard time. I have practiced this exercise and it has allowed me to continue on with my life. Here's my advice: whenever you feel stuck, indecisive, or overwhelmed due to school, emotions, or something else, do the following:

1. **Write in a journal.** It allows you to let everything out onto the page, especially the things you don't want others to know. Try writing every day or when you feel like you need a release. I personally like to write at night because it relaxes me, quiets my mind, and helps me sleep.
2. **Put yourself in a room or go to your favorite park or favorite quiet place.** Make sure to bring a notebook or paper and a pen. When you are in the spot you feel comfortable and you are alone, start writing the pros and cons of the situation, decision, or emotions you are feeling. Then read them out loud. If you have to read it more than once, do so. This helps you go through what is good, and what is not so good, but can be good for you in the end. When I come to a moment in my life where I am stuck, I practice this and I feel more peaceful and relaxed, and mentally prepared for any discord I need to face or obstacle I have to overcome.

THIS IS ME

I am Miriam Estela Bigurra, a young Latina with dreams and ambitions. I was born in Elgin, Illinois to a Mexican father and a Bolivian mother, so I proudly consider myself BoliMex, a product of two beautiful Latino cultures. I am involved in a nonprofit organization called Renacer Boliviano and I am part of Renacer Boliviano Dance Troupe. I plan on finishing my last two classes in the fall of 2020 to graduate from Colombia College with a bachelor's degree in theatre. Currently, I work as a banker at J.P. Morgan Chase. I am also happily married to an amazing husband, Aroldo Vaca, and am grateful he is part of my life and a big supporter in everything I do.

My dream is to have a successful career in performing as well be a strong and positive example for my family.

THE FIVE-YEAR PLAN

1. Apply to a social media company, TV station, or act or produce a film
2. Start up my music career
3. Buy a home and start a family

A DIFFERENT EDUCATION

Lucero Carrasco

"My character is not defined by my lack of academic excellence."

My family always told me, *"Ponte ha estudiar, para que puedas salir de la pobreza!"* (Get yourself an education so that you can get out of poverty!) Although I heard it often, it never fully stuck. Growing up, I didn't care for school as much as my parents would have liked. I sort of grazed through school, never the best and never the worst, just average.

In my junior year of high school, my family's advice totally flew out the window. I started slacking off in class, missing assignments and even ditching school. I admit that I was a spoiled, only child and even though my parents weren't wealthy, they always tried to give me everything I wanted. Maybe that was their biggest mistake…they spoiled me too much because I was their one and only. They seemed to have raised a bad kid, or at least that's what they thought at the time.

Oftentimes, parents judge their children on how well they

perform in their academics. For my parents, they were afraid I would perpetuate the stigma of the Hispanic student who doesn't graduate high school. Then, to their disgrace, I ended up dropping out after failing my senior year. My parents have always been the most important people in my life. I didn't want to disappoint them so I tried to make it up to them in other ways. I remember feeling so disappointed in myself that I wanted to find a way to make them proud of me. As a result, I started looking for a respectable, paying job.

WHITE LIES

During high school, I worked as a waitress for well-known, Chicago catering company, but I was not making a considerable amount of money because it was only a weekend job. I started applying to different jobs and eventually, I was hired at a warehouse retail store as a part-time cashier. At the age of eighteen, I had my first official job and I couldn't wait to tell my parents about it. My mother was happy for me, but my father wasn't too impressed. I could tell that he was still upset about the choices I made that led me to drop out of school.

I was always determined to prove something to him. After I left school, my father would constantly bully me about my intelligence. His mockery ignited a fire in me that made me unstoppable. I now know why I worked so hard to get where I am today; it was always to gain respect and admiration from my parents.

After just a couple months of working at my first retail

job as a cashier, I was promoted to a member service associate. I have always been a people person, and this has helped me tremendously throughout my career. After a year of working as a service associate, my boyfriend told me about how well his sister was doing in the banking industry and that he thought I would be a good fit there too. That conversation sparked my interest in wanting to work at a bank, so I started looking for teller positions with various banks in Chicago.

I took to the internet to help me spruce up my resume but when I got to the education portion, I blanked out. I didn't dare reveal that I didn't graduate from high school and risk the recruiters not calling me for an interview, so I lied. I took a chance, hoping that the HR department would not check the Chicago Public School system or ask me for a copy of my high school diploma. It's funny to me now because I learned that this usually doesn't happen. Luckily, I was only interviewed once at the bank of my choice and I was extended a job offer shortly after interviewing.

The day that I received the job offer for the part-time teller position was one of the happiest days in my life. I remember I couldn't wait to get home and tell my parents about it. I was sure that working at a bank was going to gain me credibility with them. I wanted to show them that I didn't need that high school diploma in my hand to land a job in a bank.

I actually carried the lie of graduating high school on my resume way beyond my first and second job. I just kept on hoping no one would ever notice, but the guilt I felt wouldn't subside. I remember that some nights I would dream that I was back in my old high school, retaking the classes that I had failed. It was my conscience telling me to go back to school and finish my GED.

Now, please don't think I encourage anyone to drop out of school, because I don't. I know that education can take you very far, but in my case, education was the last thing on my mind to get ahead. I wanted to show that my work ethic and dedication could take me just as far in life. At that point, going back to school wasn't an option for me; life now got in the way. I could have gone back for my GED during my time as a part-time teller, but the manager at the time wanted me to be flexible with my work schedule. Plus, I didn't want anyone at work to find out that I lied about the education portion of my resume. Since I wasn't going to pursue education, I was going to move up as much as I could in the banking industry.

During my time as a teller, my number one focus was to get to the next level in banking. I hardly ever stopped to think of all the skills I was learning along the way. During my first position at the bank, I learned about building my credit. The more I learned about credit, the more I was able to help my family and my Hispanic customers, who were usually the ones that needed the information the most. I remember that my first job as a teller was my favorite, not only because of the amazing colleagues I worked with but because I was helping the Hispanic community of McKinley Park. The customers there were mostly low-income, Hispanic workers with little knowledge of how finance worked. Not only was I finding a passion for helping people, I was also gaining confidence in myself.

THE BANKING WORLD

In the banking world, when you do well, your name gets known. Luckily, I was

Identified by a manager who was looking to hire a full-time teller supervisor. I would be working closer to home and move up a position at the bank. Once I applied, they called me for an interview and about a week later, they offered me the job. I was over the moon at the thought that I was already in management after such a short amount of time. Everything seemed to be going well, and it was, but there was always that uncertainty in me. In the back of my mind, I never felt good enough because I lacked the education that some of my peers had. That didn't stop me though. I kept on going wherever the wind carried me.

I didn't last long in the teller supervisor role before another opportunity presented itself. Once my manager decided to transfer to another bank, he reached out to me and asked me if I was willing to move to another company, and ultimately be promoted to a retail banker position. I didn't even think twice about saying yes. I thought I'd try anything that came my way, what did I have to lose? But once again, I felt insecure about the fact that I didn't have a GED, let alone a college degree. I didn't know how that would affect my chances of being hired. All I know is that I had heard great things about the bank where I could potentially start down another path.

The hiring process took over a month and I remember continually praying to get hired there. Finally, I ended up being hired by BMO Harris bank. I have been with BMO for more than five years and counting. I have learned and developed most of my skills and strengths at this bank. My first year here, I developed multi-tasking skills and the ability to remember internal support phone numbers by heart. Since my manager was also new at the time, he usually couldn't help me because he was learning the bank's policies and procedures himself. At first, I kind of regretted my decision to switch banks, but what I didn't understand at the time was that I was learning how to be independent and figure things out on my own.

After a year, I was able to do almost all the banking activities with my eyes closed. My manager trusted me so much that he would leave me in charge of one of his locations. I was practically running the location without the pay and recognition. I was growing tired of the situation, and I began looking to transfer to another location. I wasn't just looking for any branch; I was looking for bank where I would be noticed.

Then, a retail banker position opened up in the headquarters in downtown Chicago. I felt intimidated as I applied, but I went ahead and did it anyway. I would never forget how quickly everything happened. The day after they received my application, the manager called me to schedule an interview that same week. I interviewed with the manager and the assistant manager, and when the assistant manager asked me what my next step was, I basically told him that I wanted his job.

Instead of being intimidated, he told the branch manager to hire me ASAP. They extended the job offer to me the very next day. The next two years at their headquarters, which we called

"Main," would be the most important in my career at BMO.

The branch at Main was always under a microscope and you had to be on top of your game because executives were always watching. In my first two years there, there was major manager turnover; four managers came and went. One in particular taught me the real meaning of hard work.

MENTORS AND MONEY

Kelly was a strong woman, dedicated to her employees, and she had created a brand for herself in the world of banking. After she started managing me, I became inspired to be a branch manager. I remember staying late at the office with her, just to learn from her wisdom. She was only my manager for four months but she was by far the one who taught me the most about life. Before she left, she made sure to let the market manager know about my abilities. Thanks to Kelly's sponsorship, I would embark on my next journey with the bank.

The market manager asked me to oversee the branch until a new manager was put in place. Overseeing the largest branch in the U.S. made me very nervous, but I figured that if I can do it, then the rest of the branches would be a piece of cake. Since I had potential to be a manager, my market president nominated me for the Bank Manager Development program to prepare me for management.

It's funny how things work, because before Kelly started managing me, I was unmotivated and looking to leave my job. That all changed when I decided to change my attitude and try my best. Every door opened for me after that. The same year I was nominated to the management program, another branch manager, Letti, nominated me for another program named *Fuerte*.

Being a part of *Fuerte* was one of the best things that could have happened to me. Aside from the program being a training ground for young women of color, it helped me meet another mentor. Luz is the founder of Latinas on the Plaza and the Fuerte program. With her guidance, I was able to master necessary skills I needed to use in my current role as a manager. The program taught me how to be more organized when planning goals, and it gave me the confidence to speak up for myself. I met other Latina women with similar struggles and backgrounds. I knew I wasn't alone in my journey to a better

life. Because of Luz, I got the chance to write this story and share it with the world.

My character is not defined by my lack of academic excellence; just because I didn't follow the traditional path of graduating high school and going to college doesn't mean that I didn't have aspirations in life. I was educated through my various jobs, and I gained real life experiences. My work experience gave me an understanding of many things related to everyday life. Even though education was not my number one priority for many years, my grit made up for it.

Eventually, I did go back to a community college to obtain my GED and enroll in my first college class. During my journey, there were so many people I met that thought that their lack of education was a huge barrier in their lives. I always thought that if you have the will, there will always be a way to overcome any obstacle!

My experiences and "different education" now help me aspire to make a bigger difference in my community while progressing in my goals. Growing up, I heard my parents talk about money and I remember their conversations. They were always planning and talking about budgeting because they wanted to save money to be homeowners. I consider myself to be lucky to have learned money management skills since before adulthood. This is not always the case for the individuals in the Hispanic community.

I want to leave a mark in the lives of people, so when they think of me, they think of what financial goals they were able to accomplish because of my guidance. I have an immense passion for charity and volunteering and I want to be able to help people obtain financial literacy. In all my years working for a bank, I have noticed how a lack of financial literacy can keep a person in poverty. I have witnessed this firsthand with many of my own customers as I have advised them. They need a different type of education too. It can make just as big a difference in their life as it has in mine!

THINK YOUNG AND GROW

What barriers to reaching your goals are you currently facing? Write them all down. Number them with number one being your biggest priority. Then write a realistic date to complete your number one goal. It always helps when you plan way ahead of schedule because you get more time to prepare. Commit to a scheduled date of completion. You will be glad you did.

THIS IS ME

My name is Lucero Carrasco and I am a Mexican-American woman born and raised on the southside of Chicago. I am the only child to Ana and Vicente Carrasco, and a mom to a precious Yorkie Terrier named Baby. I am passionate about helping others and sharing my knowledge with those who need it. I am currently a bank manager for BMO Harris bank in the Chicagoland area. I enjoy singing, collecting National Geographic magazines, and traveling with my family. I also want to thank my family and the mentors in my life because without them, I wouldn't be where I am today. Thank you, Mom and Dad, Nina, Manny, Christina, Ricardo, Rafael, Kelly, Letti, and Luz. Your guidance and support have shaped me to be the strong independent woman I am today.

My biggest dream is to open a non-profit organization that helps people in the community with financial literacy.

THE FIVE-YEAR PLAN

1. Obtain a bachelor's degree in business administration with a minor in philanthropy
2. Become a board member at a non-profit organization
3. Work in Community Affairs

Jacqueline S. Ruíz

BIOGRAPHY

Jacqueline S. Ruiz is a visionary social entrepreneur that has created an enterprise of inspiration. Her keen sense of service coupled with the vision to bring good to the world have led her to create two successful award-winning companies, establish two nonprofit organizations, publish 19 books, create over 10 products, and has held dozens of events around the world in just the past decade.

She is often referred to as a "dream catcher" as her strategies have supported thousands of women, authors and young ladies to live a life of significance. Jacqueline's quest to be a servant leader extends to every area of her life. She has shared her inspiration in four continents and aligned with some of the most powerful brands to elevate others. At only 36 years of age, she has achieved what most would not do in an entire lifetime. Being a cancer survivor sparked a sense of urgency to serve and transcend.

Jacqueline believes that magix (yes, a made-up word that means magic x 10) is the interception of profit and impact. She is one of the few Latina sports airplane pilots in the United States and is about to embark on the historic air race that 20 women flyers participated in crossing the United States 91 years ago, including the famous Amelia Earhart.

Jacqueline believes that *"taking off is optional, landing on your dreams is mandatory."*

Alexandria Ríos Taylor

BIOGRAPHY

Alexandria Rios Taylor is a high school Assistant Principal in the southwest suburbs of Chicago. She works with youth on leadership development and career pathways. She delivers presentations which draw upon her personal experience in public education as well as research from her doctoral fieldwork. Her commitment to educational equity has served as the foundation for her conferences, workshops, and addresses. Alex is proud to be partnering with Jackie on this collaboration and is excited to be featured in the *Today's Inspired Latina series*.

Alex is currently pursuing her doctorate degree in educational administration at Aurora University as she examines the pipeline of diverse educators. She holds a master's degree in leadership and administration from Benedictine University and completed her undergraduate studies at North Central College. She double majored and earned a bachelor's degree in both organizational communication and Spanish where she received the Carleen Verstraete Award and the Rasmussen Scholarship. Alex was later recognized by her alma mater and received the Sesquicentennial Award in education as a top educator in her decade.

Although she is proud of her tenure as an educator and service to her community, nothing gives Alex more gratification than coming home to her two kids, Elena and Maceo, and her devoted husband, Gentri.

Made in the USA
Monee, IL
29 September 2020